# SIMPLE SOMATIC THERAPY SOLUTION WORKBOOK

## 30 MINUTE
### DAILY TRANSFORMATION
### with SOMATIC EXERCISES,
### Vagus Nerve Stimulation,
### & Heart Rate Variability Biofeedback
### for Trauma, Anxiety, & Depression

*Holistic Harmony*
*Publications*

# TABLE OF CONTENTS

**Emotional Overwhelm to Steady Confidence?** – Navigate life's ups and downs with powerful self-assessments and mood awareness tools.

**Negative Thought Spirals to Empowered Mindset?** – Use Rational Emotive Behavior Therapy (REBT) tools and self-talk reframing to shift your perspective and regain control.

**Crisis Mode to Calm Readiness?** – Stay prepared with a personal emergency plan and progress tracker so you can respond—not react—to emotional triggers.

**Your Emotional First Aid Toolkit is Here.**
**Simple. Science-Backed. Effective.**

**Take charge of your emotional resilience today!**
**DOWNLOAD NOW AND START YOUR TRANSFORMATION!**
**eBook:** https://simplesomatictherapy.myflodesk.com/oce5az0x6d

# FORWARD FOR SIMPLE SOMATIC THERAPY

## SOLUTION WORKBOOK

In a world that moves faster than our nervous systems can process, where stress is worn like armor and emotional overwhelm is too often dismissed as weakness, the need for grounded, body-based healing has never been more urgent, or more empowering. This book offers a lifeline: a practical, evidence-informed, and deeply compassionate guide to regulating your emotions, calming your body, and restoring balance from the inside out.

As a licensed mental health professional, I've spent years searching for effective, accessible strategies to support clients struggling with anxiety, trauma, and emotional dysregulation. Many arrive at therapy exhausted, having tried traditional talk therapy or medication, only to find that something still feels stuck. What they often need is not more analysis, but a way back into their bodies.

That's where NeuroSomatic Therapy, the foundation of this workbook, has transformed the way I approach healing. In my clinical practice, I've witnessed the remarkable impact of somatic techniques, vagus nerve stimulation, and heart rate variability (HRV) biofeedback. These methods don't just manage symptoms, they reshape how the brain and body respond to stress. They offer real relief, and more importantly, real agency.

What you hold in your hands is more than a collection of tools; it's a roadmap to reconnecting with your most powerful resource: yourself. The 30-minute daily practices are designed to be simple, science-backed, and incredibly effective. No special equipment, no clinical training, just you, your breath, your awareness, and your willingness to begin.

This book doesn't ask you to talk your way out of pain. Instead, it gently invites you to feel your way through it. With each grounding technique, breathwork session, and mindful movement practice, you'll tap into the innate intelligence of your nervous system. You'll learn to create safety within, regulate your emotions in real time, and build resilience that lasts.

Healing doesn't always start with big breakthroughs. Sometimes, it begins with a single pause. A breath. A choice to notice. Each chapter of this workbook guides you through practical, restorative experiences—complete with reflection prompts and tracking tools—to help you cultivate a personalized practice of self-regulation and healing. Let this book be your companion. May it offer not just strategies, but hope. Not just calm, but connection. Not just relief, but a return to yourself.

To your healing,
**Melissa Ginest, MA, LPC**
*Adolescent and Trauma Specialist*

# SOMATIC DAILY GROUNDING TECHNIQUES

**Welcome!** Let's take a moment to pause. Life can feel like a whirlwind, can't it? With work, family, never-ending to-do lists, and the constant ping of notifications, it's easy to feel cut off from ourselves. However, here's a little-known fact: your body can be a strong anchor to help you stay in the present moment. That's where somatic therapy comes in.

Grounding can be thought of as a reset button for your inner world. Imagine you were a tree; grounding would enable your roots to penetrate deeply into the ground, giving you stability regardless of how powerful the winds are. When your thoughts are disorganized, or your emotions feel too much to handle, grounding practices can help you focus on the present.

Perhaps you've experienced feeling "off-center" or "stuck in your head" before. That is quite typical. Using easy, efficient techniques that emphasize your body and senses, these grounding exercises can help you regain your balance. You could focus on the feel of your feet on the ground, the rhythm of your breathing, or even the sense of an object in your palm.

Here's an example: You've had a hectic day. You missed lunch, you have a ton of deadlines, and your mind is racing. Instead of spiraling further, you stop and rest your hands on your thighs. You inhale deeply, feeling the firm support of the chair underneath you. You let yourself be for a few seconds.

These brief periods of grounding can have a significant impact. They're not just about "calming down." They are about tuning in and regaining your sense of security and stability. Ready to explore these techniques? Let's start—you'll discover how to stay grounded in the present moment regardless of what life throws at you!

# DAILY GROUNDING TECHNIQUES

Grounding techniques work differently from traditional therapies by focusing on the physiological level. While talk therapy addresses the cognitive and emotional aspects, grounding techniques engage the body and nervous system to promote immediate relief.

Imagine feeling a wave of anxiety coming on; instead of getting caught in a spiral of negative thoughts, grounding techniques help you focus on the here and now. By doing so, they interrupt the cycle of anxiety and provide a tangible way to manage symptoms.

These simple yet powerful methods offer immediate and long-term emotional regulation and healing benefits.

## The 5-4-3-2-1 Technique

**Purpose:** The 5-4-3-2-1 Technique is one of several grounding methods that can be particularly effective, as it engages the senses to bring you back to the present moment.

You start by listing five things you can see, four things you can touch, three things you can hear, two things you can smell, and one thing you can taste. This sensory engagement helps distract your mind from anxious thoughts and focuses your attention on your surroundings.

Over time, practicing this technique can enhance your ability to stay present and emotionally regulated.

1. **Find a Comfortable Position:** Sit or stand in a relaxed position and take a deep breath to begin.

2. **Name Five Things You Can See:** Look around and slowly name five things you can see. Say them out loud or in your mind, focusing on the details.

3. **Identify Four Things You Can Touch:** Notice four things you can physically touch around you. Feel their textures and sensations with your hands.

4. **Listen for Three Sounds:** Close your eyes if comfortable and listen. Identify three sounds you can hear, whether they're loud, soft, close, or far away.

5. **Notice Two Things You Can Smell:** Take a deep breath and identify two distinct smells. If nothing stands out, focus on the air you breathe in or use a scented item like lotion.

6. **Recognize One Thing You Can Taste:** Pay attention to your mouth and identify one taste. If needed, take a sip of water or chew gum to help with this step.

7. **Repeat as Needed:** Continue this process until you feel calmer and more grounded in the present moment.

# How to Use the Mood Thermometer

This thermometer helps you track your emotional intensity or stress level. Take a moment to check in with yourself and rate how you're feeling on a scale from 0 to 10.

- 0-2 (Green): Calm, relaxed, or at ease.

- 3-6 (Yellow): A bit uneasy, stressed, or neutral.

- 7-10 (Red): Overwhelmed, anxious, or distressed.

Mark your number on the thermometer to identify your current state. Use this tool daily or during tough moments to better understand your emotions and find ways to manage them.

# Step-by-Step Guide 5-4-3-2-1 Technique

Use this space to guide yourself through the technique. Follow each step and jot down your observations.

## Find a Comfortable Position

Describe your posture: _____

0  1  2  3  4  5  6  7  8  9  10

Notice 5 things that you can see. Look around you. Observe and write down five things that you can see.

Notice 4 things that you can feel. Tune in to your sense of touch. Notice and describe the texture of four things you can touch.

Notice 3 things that you can hear. Listen carefully. Notice and write down three sounds you hear in your environment.

Notice 2 things that you can smell. Notice and write down two smells you recognize.

Notice 1 thing that you can taste. Focus and write down one thing that you can taste right now.

# Daily Practice Log

| | |
|---|---|
| **Date & Time of Day** | |
| **Initial Anxiety Level (1-10)** | |
| **Post-Exercise Anxiety Level (1-10)** | |
| **Initial Heart Rate Variability** | |
| **Post-Exercise Heart Rate Variability** | |
| **Notes on Experience** | |

# Reflection

**How do you feel now? (Rate your anxiety again on a scale of 1-10)**

**Did you notice any changes in your emotional state?**

**Was there a specific sense that was most grounding for you? Why?**

# PHYSICAL GROUNDING TECHNIQUES

**Purpose:** Physical grounding techniques, such as touching a textured object, stomping your feet, or walking barefoot in nature, can be highly effective in reconnecting you with your body and the physical world. These methods provide immediate relief from anxiety and promote long-term emotional stability. For example, holding a grounding object, like a stress ball, and focusing on its texture can help anchor you in the present moment. Similarly, pressing your feet firmly into the ground can enhance your sense of connection. Over time, these techniques can improve your ability to regulate emotions and stay grounded during stressful situations.

1. **Choose a Grounding Object:** Find a small object with a distinct texture, such as a stress ball, stone, or fabric. Keep it nearby for easy access when you feel anxious.

2. **Focus on Texture:** Hold the object in your hand and focus on its texture. Notice its temperature, weight, and how it feels in your palm. Move your fingers over its surface and pay attention to every sensation.

3. **Press Your Feet into the Ground:** Press your feet firmly into the ground while sitting or standing. Feel the connection between your feet and the surface beneath you. Wiggle your toes and notice how the ground supports you.

4. **Engage Your Senses:** If possible, walk barefoot on a natural surface like grass or sand. Feel the textures and temperatures as you walk, focusing on each step.

5. **Breathe and Notice:** Take slow, deep breaths while focusing on the sensations in your hands or feet. This will help you stay present and enhance the grounding effect.

6. **Repeat as Needed:** Use these physical grounding techniques whenever you feel overwhelmed. With regular practice, they can become a reliable tool for managing stress and anxiety.

# Worksheet: Physical Grounding Techniques

- **Objective:** Use this worksheet to guide your practice of physical grounding techniques, helping you reconnect with your body and the present moment during times of stress or anxiety.
- **Benefits:** Provides immediate relief from overwhelming emotions, enhances emotional stability, and strengthens mind-body awareness with consistent use.

## Step-by-Step Guide

### 1. Choose a Grounding Object

| What object did you choose (e.g., stress ball, stone, fabric)? | Why did you choose this object? |
| --- | --- |
| | |

### 2. Focus on Texture

| Describe the object's texture (e.g., rough, smooth, soft, hard): | Note other details (e.g., temperature, weight, shape): |
| --- | --- |
| | |

## 3. Press Your Feet into the Ground

**Were you sitting or standing? & Describe the sensation of your feet pressing into the ground** (e.g., firmness, stability)

**Did you wiggle your toes? How did that feel?**

## 4. Engage Your Senses

**Did you walk barefoot? Yes / No & What surface did you walk on** (e.g., grass, sand, carpet)?

**Describe the sensations in your feet as you walked** (e.g., soft, cool, warm, gritty):

## 5. Breathe and Notice

**Describe how your body felt as you breathed deeply while focusing on your hands or feet:**

**How many breaths did you take? & Did you notice any shift in your emotional or physical state?**

## 6. Repeat as Needed

**How long did you practice this technique?**

**Optional: Rate your anxiety before and after the exercise on a scale of 1-10.**

# Daily Practice Log

| | |
|---|---|
| **Date & Time of Day** | |
| **Duration of Practice** | |
| **Stress or anxiety level before and after practice (1-10)** | |
| **Initial Heart Rate Variability** | |
| **Post-Exercise Heart Rate Variability** | |
| **What physical grounding technique did you use? & What sensations or emotions did you notice during practice?** | |
| **Additional Notes** | |

# Reflection Questions

**Which technique felt most effective today (e.g., holding an object, pressing feet, walking barefoot)? Why?**

**Did you encounter any challenges while practicing? How can you address them?**

**How can you incorporate physical grounding into your daily routine?**

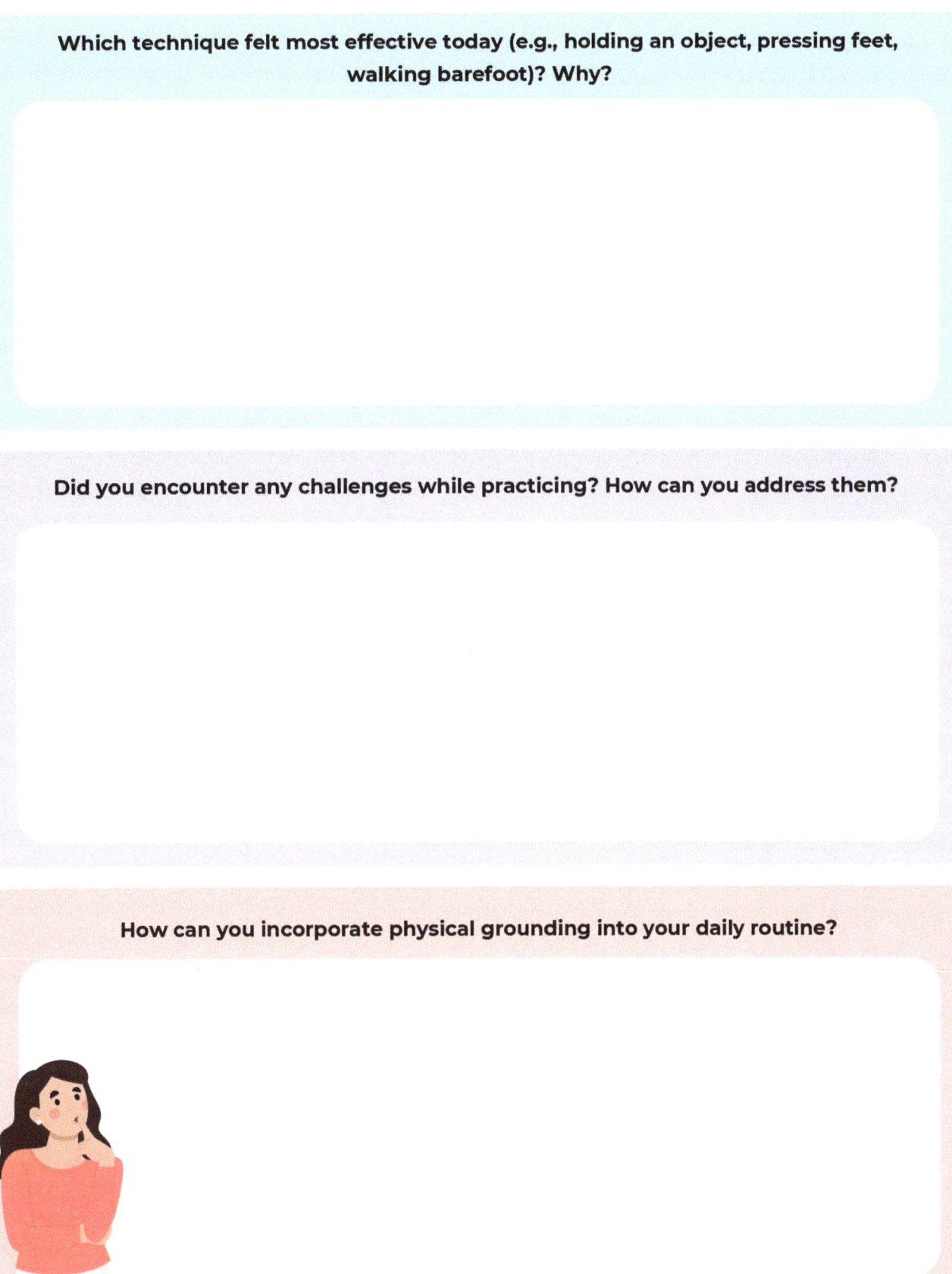

# Weekly Self-Assessment

Complete this section at the end of the week to reflect on your progress.

How many times did you practice physical grounding this week?

What was the most grounding object or surface for you? Why?

Did you notice changes in your ability to regulate emotions? Describe them:

What are your goals for practicing physical grounding next week?

# DEEP BELLY BREATHING TECHNIQUE

**Purpose:** Deep Belly Breathing, also known as diaphragmatic breathing, is another effective grounding technique. This method involves breathing deeply into your diaphragm, which stimulates the vagus nerve and activates the parasympathetic nervous system and promotes relaxation. When you breathe deeply, you send a signal to your brain that it's safe to relax, reducing anxiety and stress. This technique provides immediate calming effects and, with regular practice, helps manage stress and trauma over the long term.

1. **Find a Comfortable Position:** Sit or lie down in a relaxed position, placing one hand on your chest and the other on your abdomen.

2. **Inhale Slowly:** Breathe deeply through your nose for a count of four. Focus on expanding your abdomen as you inhale rather than your chest. You should feel the hand on your abdomen rise while the hand on your chest remains still.

3. **Hold Your Breath:** Gently hold your breath for a count of two to let the air settle into your diaphragm.

4. **Exhale Slowly:** Breathe out through your mouth for a count of six, feeling your abdomen fall as you release the air. Make a soft "whoosh" sound as you exhale to enhance the relaxation effect.

5. **Repeat this process** for 5-10 breaths or until you feel more relaxed and grounded. Practice regularly to strengthen your body's relaxation response.

## Diaphragmatic Breathing

**Position:** Sit or lie down comfortably, hands on your abdomen.

**Inhale:** Slowly breathe in through your nose for 4 counts, expanding your stomach.

**Hold:** Hold the breath for 2 counts.

**Exhale:** Exhale through your mouth for 6 counts, feeling your stomach fall.

**Repeat:** 5-10 breaths.

## What did you notice during this practice?

# Worksheet: Deep Belly Breathing Practice

- **Objective:** Use this worksheet to guide your practice of Deep Belly Breathing and track its effects on your emotional and physical state.
- **Benefits:** Activates the parasympathetic nervous system, reduces stress, and promotes a state of calm. Regular practice enhances long-term resilience to stress and trauma.

## Step-by-Step Guide

### 1. Find a Comfortable Position

| Describe your position: | Optional: Rate your stress or anxiety level before starting on a scale of 1-10. |
|---|---|
| | |

## 2. Inhale Slowly

| | |
|---|---|
| Note how it feels to expand your abdomen | Did your chest remain still? Yes / No   |

## 3. Hold Your Breath

Describe any sensations during the breath hold (e.g., tension, calm, discomfort)

## 4. Exhale Slowly

| | |
|---|---|
| How does your body feel as you exhale? | Did you make the soft "whoosh" sound? Yes / No   |

## 5. Repeat for 5-10 Breaths

| Breath 1 | Breath 5 | Breath 10 |
|---|---|---|
| Stress Level | Stress Level | Stress Level |
| Noted Feeling | Noted Feeling | Noted Feeling |

# Daily Practice Log

| | |
|---|---|
| **Date & Time of Day** | |
| **How long did you practice?** | |
| **What was your initial stress or anxiety level (1-10)?** | |
| **What was your stress or anxiety level after practice (1-10)?** | |
| **Initial Heart Rate Variability** | |
| **Post-Exercise Heart Rate Variability** | |
| **Additional Notes** | |

# Reflection Questions

Did you notice any changes in your breathing or emotional state?

Was there a specific part of the exercise that felt particularly effective or challenging?

How can you integrate this technique into your daily routine?

# Weekly Self-Assessment

Complete this section at the end of the week to track your progress.

**How many times did you practice Deep Belly Breathing this week?**

**What patterns or changes did you notice?**

**How has your stress or anxiety level changed overall?**

**What are your goals for next week's practice?**

# MENTAL GROUNDING TECHNIQUES

**Purpose:** Mental grounding techniques, such as counting backward from 100, can effectively shift your focus away from anxiety or panic. This mentally engaging activity provides immediate relief by distracting you from distressing thoughts and emotions. Over time, practicing this technique can enhance your ability to manage anxiety and racing thoughts more effectively.

1. **Find a Quiet Space:** Sit or stand in a comfortable, quiet space where you can focus without interruptions.

2. **Take a Deep Breath:** Before you begin, take a slow, deep breath to help center yourself.

3. **Start Counting:** Slowly start counting backward from 100. Say each number out loud or in your mind, focusing your attention on each one as you go.

4. **Visualize Each Number:** As you count, try to picture each number in your mind. This added mental imagery can help further distract you from anxious thoughts.

5. **Slow Down if Needed:** If you find your mind wandering back to anxiety, slow down your counting. You can even pause between numbers to deepen the calming effect.

6. **Repeat as Needed:** Continue counting backward until you notice decreased anxiety. You can repeat this exercise whenever you feel overwhelmed to help manage distressing thoughts.

# Worksheet: Mental Grounding Techniques

- **Objective:** Use this worksheet to practice mental grounding techniques, such as counting backward from 100, to distract your mind from distressing thoughts and regain a sense of calm.
- **Benefits:** Provides immediate relief from anxiety, improves focus, and helps manage racing thoughts over time.

## Step-by-Step Guide

| | |
|---|---|
| 1. Find a Quiet Space: Where did you choose to practice (e.g., bedroom, office, park)? | 2. Take a Deep Breath: Describe how you felt after taking a slow, deep breath (e.g., more centered, still anxious): |

### 3. Start Counting

| | |
|---|---|
| Did you count out loud or in your mind? | How far did you get before noticing a shift in your focus or emotions? |

## 4. Visualize Each Number

| | |
|---|---|
| **Did you picture the numbers in your mind? Yes / No**  | **Describe how you visualized the numbers (e.g., colors, shapes, sizes):** |

## 5. Slow Down if Needed

| | |
|---|---|
| **If so, did slowing down help? What did you notice?** | **Did you find your mind wandering back to anxiety? Yes / No** 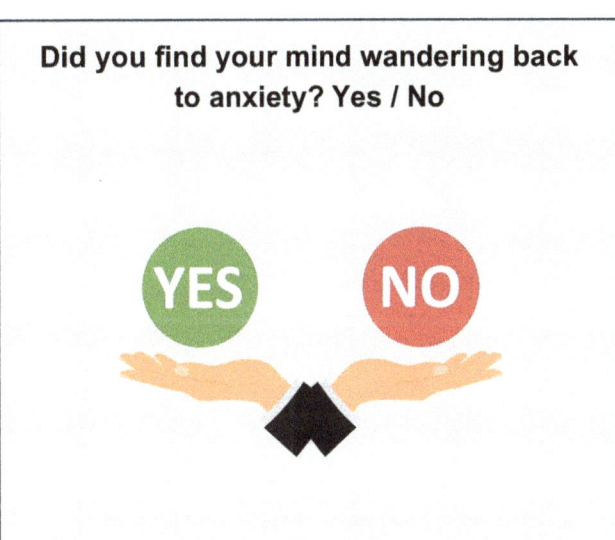 |

## 6. Repeat as Needed

| | |
|---|---|
| **How long did you practice this technique?** | **Optional: Rate your anxiety before and after the exercise on a scale of 1-10.** |

# Daily Practice Log

| | |
|---|---|
| **Date &<br>Time of Day** | |
| **How far did you count during this session?** | |
| **Stress or anxiety level before and after practice (1-10** | |
| **Initial Heart Rate Variability** | |
| **Post-Exercise Heart Rate Variability** | |
| **What helped you stay focused on counting (e.g., visualizing numbers, slowing down)?** | |
| **Additional Notes** | |

# Reflection Questions

What was most effective about this technique for you today?

Did you encounter any challenges while practicing (e.g., distractions, difficulty visualizing)?

How did your emotions or physical state change during or after the exercise?

How can you incorporate this technique into your routine (e.g., during stressful moments, daily check-ins)?

# Weekly Self-Assessment

Complete this section at the end of the week to reflect on your progress.

**How many times did you practice mental grounding this week?**

**Did counting backward help reduce your anxiety or distress? Describe your experience:**

**Have you noticed any improvements in managing racing thoughts or staying focused?**

**What adjustments would make this technique even more effective for you?**

# SENSORY GROUNDING TECHNIQUES

**Purpose:** Sensory grounding techniques, such as aromatherapy, listening to calming music, or focusing on the sounds around you, can quickly reduce anxiety symptoms and help you reconnect with the present moment. Engaging your senses in this way provides immediate relief and promotes long-term emotional healing. For instance, calming music can soothe your mind and body, offering a break from anxious thoughts.

1. **Choose a Sense to Focus On:** Decide whether you want to engage your sense of smell, sound, or touch. You can also combine multiple senses if that feels helpful.

2. **Aromatherapy:** If using aromatherapy, select a calming scent such as lavender, eucalyptus, or chamomile. Place a drop of essential oil on a cotton ball or use a diffuser. Take slow, deep breaths, focusing on the scent as you inhale.

3. **Listen to Calming Music:** Find a piece of calming music or nature sounds. Close your eyes and focus on the rhythm, melody, or individual instruments. Let the sound wash over you, pulling your attention away from anxious thoughts.

4. **Tune into Surrounding Sounds:** If using the sounds around you, close your eyes and take a moment to listen. Identify and focus on different sounds, like birds chirping, distant conversations, or the hum of a fan.

5. **Notice Physical Sensations:** If you are engaging in touch, grab a soft or textured item, like a blanket or stress ball. Focus on how it feels against your skin, noticing every detail.

6. **Repeat as Needed:** Continue the sensory grounding for as long as needed. Practice regularly to enhance your ability to manage anxiety and improve your overall emotional resilience. Over time, you will find these techniques more accessible to access, allowing you to ground yourself more quickly in challenging situations.

# Worksheet: Sensory Grounding Techniques

- **Objective:** Use this worksheet to guide and track your practice of sensory grounding techniques. These exercises help you reconnect with the present moment by engaging your senses.
- **Benefits:** Reduces anxiety, provides immediate emotional relief, and enhances long-term emotional resilience.

## Step-by-Step Guide

### 1. Choose a Sense to Focus On

Which sense(s) did you choose to engage today? (Check all that apply):

- [ ] Smell
- [ ] Sound
- [ ] Touch
- [ ] Sight
- [ ] Taste

### 2. Describe Your Setup

| If you used aromatherapy, which scent did you select? (e.g., lavender, eucalyptus, chamomile, or other). | If you listened to music or sounds, what did you choose? (e.g., calming music, nature sounds, a specific playlist). | If you focused on touch, what item or texture did you engage with? (e.g., blanket, stress ball, soft fabric): |
|---|---|---|
|  |  |  |

## 3. Sensory Focus Exercise

| | |
|---|---|
| **What specific sensations or details did you notice? (e.g., the coolness of the scent, the rhythm of the music)** | **Time Spent: How long did you spend practicing this technique? (e.g., 5 minutes, 10 minutes)** |

## 4. Immediate Emotional Response

On a scale of 1–10 (1 = highly anxious, 10 = very calm), how did you feel before starting this exercise?

On the same scale, how did you feel after completing the exercise?

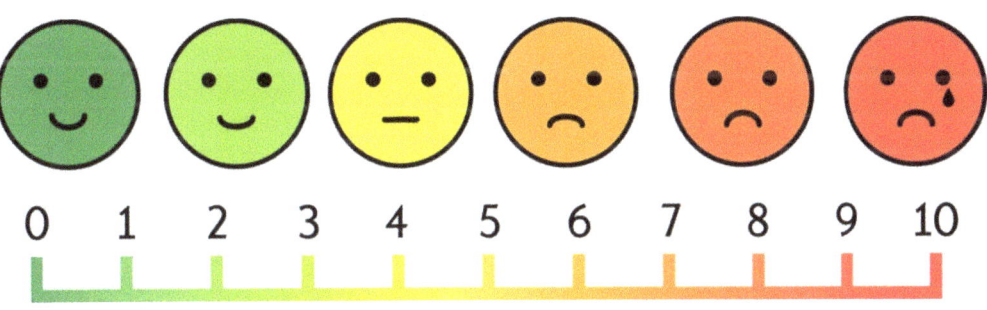

# Reflection Questions

**What did you find most helpful about this practice today?**

**Did any particular sense feel more grounding than others? Why?**

**What will you do differently (if anything) next time?**

# Practice Log

| Date | Technique Practiced | Initial Heart Rate Variability | Post-Exercise Heart Rate Variability | Notes/Observations |
|------|---------------------|--------------------------------|--------------------------------------|--------------------|
|      |                     |                                |                                      |                    |

## ADDITIONAL TIPS

Try different combinations of senses to discover which ones work best for you.

Keep this worksheet handy for future reference, and use it as a tool to track your progress over time.

**Remember:** Sensory grounding is most effective when practiced regularly, even during calm periods. This builds resilience and prepares you for challenging moments.

# WALKING GROUNDING

**Purpose:** Walking grounding involves slow, intentional movement to reconnect with your body and environment. This technique provides immediate relief from restlessness or anxiety and promotes long-term presence and emotional regulation. By focusing on the physical sensations of walking, you can anchor yourself in the present moment and reduce anxiety.

1. **Find a Safe Space:** Choose a quiet, safe area where you can walk uninterrupted, either indoors or outdoors.

2. **Start Slowly:** Begin walking at a slow, comfortable pace. Let your arms hang naturally at your sides, and focus on each step.

3. **Focus on Sensations:** Pay close attention to the physical sensations as you walk. Notice how your feet make contact with the ground, how your legs move, and how your body shifts with each step.

4. **Engage Your Senses:** As you walk, observe your surroundings. Notice what you see, hear, and smell. Feel the texture of the ground beneath your feet, whether it's grass, pavement, or carpet.

5. **Sync with Your Breath:** Take deep, slow breaths as you walk. Inhale through your nose, feel the air fill your lungs, and exhale through your mouth, syncing your breathing with your steps.

6. **Repeat as Needed:** Continue this mindful walking for several minutes or until you feel more grounded. Use this technique whenever you need to reconnect with your body and the present moment.

# Worksheet: Walking Grounding Practice

- **Objective:** Use this worksheet to guide your practice of walking grounding. This exercise helps reduce anxiety and restlessness by anchoring your focus on the sensations of walking and your connection to the present moment.
- **Benefits:** Provides immediate relief from stress, enhances physical and emotional awareness, and promotes long-term emotional regulation.

## Step-by-Step Guide

### 1. Find a Safe Space

| Where did you choose to walk (e.g., park, hallway, backyard)? | Was this space free of interruptions? |
|---|---|
| |  |

### 2. Focus on Sensations

| What physical sensations did you notice as you walked (e.g., feet touching the ground, body movements)? | How would you describe your posture and balance? |
|---|---|
| | |

# 3. Engage Your Senses

| | | | |
|---|---|---|---|
| What did you see during your walk (e.g., trees, walls, objects)? | What did you hear (e.g., birds, footsteps, distant noises)? | What did you smell (e.g., fresh air, flowers, or neutral odors)? | What textures did you feel under your feet (e.g., grass, pavement, carpet)? |

# 5. Sync with Your Breath

Did you sync your breath with your steps? Yes / No & Describe your breathing pattern (e.g., deep, shallow, steady):

Did syncing your breath with your steps help you feel more connected?

# 6. Repeat as Needed

| How long did you practice walking grounding? | Optional: Rate your stress or anxiety level before and after the exercise on a scale of 1-10 |
|---|---|

# Daily Practice Log

| | |
|---|---|
| **Date &<br>Time of Day** | |
| **Where did you walk?** | |
| **Stress or anxiety level before<br>and after practice (1-10)** | |
| **Initial Heart Rate Variability** | |
| **Post-Exercise Heart Rate<br>Variability** | |
| **What sensations or emotions<br>did you notice during<br>practice?** | |
| **Additional Notes** | |

# Reflection Questions

What did you notice most during your walk today (e.g., sensations, surroundings, emotions)?

Did any particular part of the exercise feel especially grounding or calming?

Were there any challenges (e.g., distractions, difficulty focusing)? How can you overcome them?

How can you incorporate walking grounding into your daily routine (e.g., after work, during breaks)?

# Weekly Self-Assessment

Complete this section at the end of the week to reflect on your progress.

How many times did you practice walking grounding this week?

What was the most effective aspect of walking grounding for you?

Have you noticed changes in your ability to regulate anxiety or stay present?

What adjustments would make this technique even more effective?

# TEMPERATURE CHANGES

**Purpose:** Temperature changes can also be an effective grounding method, such as holding cold or warm objects. Sudden temperature shifts can refocus your attention away from distressing emotions and provide immediate relief. For example, having an ice cube in your hand can bring your focus to the cold sensation, distracting you from anxious thoughts.

1. **Choose Your Object:** Select a temperature-based object to use, such as an ice cube, a cold drink, a warm mug, or a heating pad.

2. **Hold the Object:** Place the chosen object in your hand. If using an ice cube, hold it in your palm and let the cold sensation spread. If using a warm object, feel the heat radiating through your hand.

3. **Focus on the Sensation:** Direct your full attention to the sensation of the cold or warmth. Notice how your skin reacts to the temperature and feels against your hand.

4. **Take Deep Breaths:** Take slow, deep breaths while holding the object. Inhale through your nose, feeling the cool or warm air, and exhale through your mouth.

5. **Engage Other Senses:** If helpful, describe the sensation to yourself. For example, say, "I feel the coldness spreading across my palm," or "The warmth is soothing and relaxing."

6. **Repeat as Needed:** Hold the object until you feel more grounded. Use this technique whenever you need a quick distraction from anxiety or distressing emotions.

## Worksheet: Temperature Changes Grounding Technique

Use this worksheet to guide and track your practice of temperature-based grounding techniques. These exercises help you refocus your attention away from distressing emotions by engaging with sudden temperature changes.
**Benefits:**
- Reduces anxiety and emotional distress
- Provides immediate grounding
- Promotes present-moment awareness

# Step-by-Step Guide

## 1. Choose Your Object

What temperature-based object did you select? (e.g., ice cube, cold drink, warm mug, heating pad):

## 2. Choose Your Object

Which hand did you use to hold the object?

- ☐ Left hand
- ☐ Right hand
- ☐ Both hands

Describe how the object felt in your hand initially

## 3. Focus on the Sensation

What did you notice about the temperature (e.g., cold spreading, warmth radiating)?

How did your skin react to the sensation?: (e.g., tingling, numbing, soothing warmth)?

## 4. Take Deep Breaths

Did you pair the exercise with deep breathing.

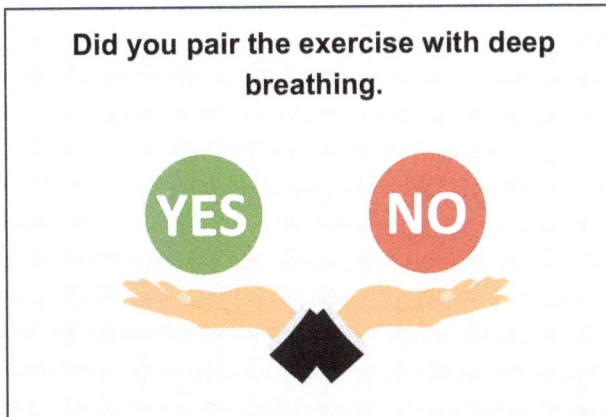

YES    NO

How did the temperature influence your breathing pattern (e.g., slowed down, deeper inhales)?

## 5. Engage Other Senses

| Did you describe the sensation to yourself? | If yes, what did you say? (e.g., "The coldness feels sharp and refreshing"): |
|---|---|
| 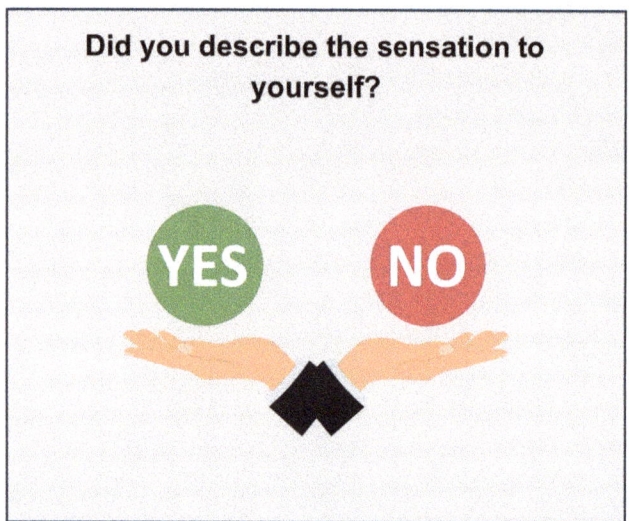 | |

## 6. Time Spent

How long did you spend on this exercise? (e.g., 2 minutes, 5 minutes):

## 7. Immediate Emotional Response

| On a scale of 1–10 (1 = highly anxious, 10 = very calm), how did you feel before starting this exercise? | On the same scale, how did you feel after completing the exercise? |
|---|---|
| | |

# Reflection Questions

**What was the most helpful aspect of this practice?**

**Did the temperature shift effectively distract you from distressing emotions? Why or why not?**

**What will you adjust for next time?**

# Practice Log

| Date | Temperature Object Used | Duration of Practice | Initial Heart Rate Variability | Post-Exercise Heart Rate Variability | Notes/ Observations |
|------|------------------------|---------------------|-------------------------------|-------------------------------------|--------------------|
|      |                        |                     |                               |                                     |                    |

## ADDITIONAL TIPS

- Experiment with different temperatures and objects to find what works best for you.

- Practice regularly to build familiarity with this grounding technique, even during calm moments.

- Combine this technique with other sensory grounding methods for a more comprehensive approach to emotional regulation.

# CREATIVE GROUNDING METHODS

**Purpose:** Creative Grounding Methods, such as drawing, painting, diamond art painting, or journaling, can also be highly effective. Engaging in creative activities helps focus your mind and express emotions, offering immediate relief from anxiety or trauma-related symptoms. These activities also promote long-term emotional regulation and healing, fostering mindfulness and a deeper connection to the present moment.

1. **Choose Your Activity:** Select a creative activity that appeals to you, such as drawing, painting, diamond art, or journaling. Keep your supplies easily accessible for when you need them.

2. **Set Up Your Space:** Find a quiet, comfortable place to focus on your chosen activity. Arrange your supplies in front of you, taking a moment to appreciate the colors, textures, or tools you'll be using.

3. **Begin Slowly:** Start your creative process slowly. If you're drawing or painting, begin with simple strokes or shapes. For journaling, start by writing down whatever comes to mind without judgment. If using diamond art, focus on placing one gem at a time.

4. **Engage Your Senses:** Pay close attention to the sensations involved in your activity. Notice the feel of the pen or brush in your hand, the sound of the pencil on the paper, or the texture of the gems.

5. **Express Your Feelings:** Use this time to express your emotions through your art or writing. Let your thoughts and feelings flow onto the paper or canvas, allowing the process to help you release tension.

6. **Focus on the Present:** Keep your mind focused on the task at hand. If your thoughts drift, gently bring your attention back to the activity.

7. **Repeat as Needed:** Continue the creative grounding until you feel more relaxed and centered. Use this technique whenever you need to reconnect with yourself and the present moment.

# PERSONALIZED GROUNDING TECHNIQUES

**Purpose:** Personalized grounding techniques can be tailored to suit individual needs, trauma histories, or specific triggers. For trauma survivors, veterans, and individuals with chronic anxiety, it's important to customize these techniques to ensure they are safe and effective. For example, a trauma survivor might find relief in physical grounding during a panic attack. At the same time, a veteran might use mental grounding techniques to manage flashbacks. Adapting these techniques based on personal experiences ensures they provide the most benefit.

1. **Identify Your Needs:** Take a moment to reflect on your specific triggers and the symptoms you experience, such as anxiety, flashbacks, or panic attacks. Understanding your unique situation will help you choose the most effective grounding techniques.

2. **Experiment with Different Methods:** Try various grounding techniques, such as physical (e.g., holding an object), mental (e.g., counting backward), or sensory (e.g., listening to calming music). Pay attention to how each method makes you feel.

3. **Assess What Works:** After trying different techniques, note which ones provide the most immediate relief and sense of calm. Consider when and how each technique is most effective, such as during moments of anxiety or flashbacks.

4. **Create a Grounding Plan:** Create a personalized grounding plan based on what works best for you. Include specific techniques you find helpful and decide when to use each one. For example, use physical grounding during panic attacks or mental grounding for racing thoughts.

5. **Practice Regularly:** Incorporate your chosen techniques into your daily routine, even when not experiencing distress. Regular practice helps strengthen your ability to use these methods effectively during stressful situations.

6. **Adjust as Needed:** Over time, reassess your grounding plan. Modify your techniques as your needs change, ensuring they remain effective and supportive of your emotional well-being.

# Worksheet: Creative and Personalized Grounding Methods

Creative and personalized grounding methods combine the benefits of engaging in artistic activities with customized approaches to grounding. These methods focus your mind, provide emotional expression, and offer tailored relief from anxiety, trauma-related symptoms, or other distressing emotions.

**Benefits:**

- Enhances mindfulness and present-moment awareness
- Provides a safe, creative outlet for emotions
- Promotes long-term emotional regulation and healing

## Step-by-Step Guide

### 1. Choose Your Activity

What creative activity do you want to try? (e.g., drawing, painting, journaling, diamond art):

If personalizing, which grounding technique suits your current needs? (e.g., physical, mental, sensory).

### 2. Identify Your Needs

What emotions, triggers, or symptoms are you addressing with this practice? (e.g., anxiety, flashbacks, racing thoughts).

## 3. Set Up Your Space

Are your creative supplies ready? (e.g., pencils, paint, journal, tools for diamond art):

Is your space quiet and comfortable? (e.g., dim lighting, soothing environment):

## 4. Begin Slowly

For creative grounding: What are you starting with? (e.g., sketching shapes, writing free thoughts, placing gems one by one):

For personalized grounding: What specific technique are you using? (e.g., holding an object, counting backward, listening to calming music):

## 5. Engage Your Senses

What sensations did you notice during your activity? (e.g., the feel of the brush, the sound of the pencil, the warmth of an object):

## 6. Express Your Feelings

If applicable, how did you express your emotions through your activity? (e.g., colors used, thoughts written, physical sensations felt):

## 7. Assess What Works

Which part of this exercise was most grounding or helpful? (e.g., focusing on art, expressing feelings, using a specific technique):

Did any part feel less effective or challenging?

## 8. Create a Personalized Plan

Based on your experience today, which techniques will you incorporate into your routine?

When will you use these techniques? (e.g., during anxiety, before bed, when feeling triggered)?

# Reflection Questions

Rate before and after on a scale of 1–10, with 1 being highly anxious and 10 being very calm.

What will you do differently next time to enhance this practice?

46

# Practice Log

| Date | Creative Activity or Grounding Technique Used | Duration of Practice | Initial Heart Rate Variability | Post-Exercise Heart Rate Variability | Notes/ Observations |
|---|---|---|---|---|---|
|  |  |  |  |  |  |

## ADDITIONAL TIPS

- Keep your supplies and plan accessible for moments of need.

- Experiment with different combinations of creative and grounding techniques to discover what works best.

- Regular practice enhances the effectiveness of these methods, even during calm periods.

# ELEVATING AWARENESS AND RELAXATION THROUGH BODY SCANNING

Have you ever observed how your body retains tension even after the day's stress has passed? Perhaps it's a tense jaw following a difficult talk, stiff shoulders following long desk work, or an unexplained queasy feeling in your stomach. Our bodies often bear the burden of events we haven't had time to digest. That's where body scanning comes in, like giving your body and mind a much-needed status check.

Consider body scanning as an exploration of your entire body, from your head to your toes. It's a simple exercise that encourages you to objectively observe your body's processes, one part at a time. Maybe your legs feel light or your shoulders weighty. Perhaps you feel warm hands or a flutter in your chest. Whatever you observe is perfectly okay—the goal isn't to change anything; it's to notice.

Let's try a quick example. Picture yourself resting after a long day. Closing your eyes, you start by focusing on your head. How does it feel? Nervous? Indifferent? You breathe deeply as you gradually shift your focus to your neck and, eventually, your shoulders. Scanning down to your feet makes you feel lighter and more in the moment. Body scanning promotes connection as much as relaxation. It helps you identify the areas of your body where stress is stored so it can be released. Additionally, it improves your self-awareness, which might help you respond to life's challenges with greater calm and clarity.

Body scanning is a gift you give to yourself, whether you're using it to relax before bed, center yourself at a difficult time, or develop a deeper sense of self-awareness. Explore this exercise at your own pace; it's a practice that meets you right where you are and allows you to reset, recharge, and reconnect with your entire self.

# BODY SCANNING

**Purpose:** Body scanning can be adapted to suit individual needs, offering flexibility in practice. A 5-minute body scan can provide rapid relaxation and increased bodily awareness for a quick daily routine. This shorter version focuses on key areas of tension, allowing you to identify and release stress quickly. For deeper relaxation, an extended 30-minute body scan offers a more thorough exploration of bodily sensations. This extended practice allows you to spend more time on each body part, promoting a deeper sense of relaxation and connection. By tailoring the practice to your needs, you can ensure that body scanning remains an effective tool for your mental and physical health.

1. **Find a Comfortable Position:** Sit or lie down in a quiet space where you won't be disturbed. Close your eyes and take a few deep breaths to center yourself.
2. **Start at the Top of Your Head:** Begin by bringing your attention to the top of your head. Notice any sensations—discomfort, tightness, warmth, or tingling, for example, tightness in your forehead or heaviness in your chest; stay present with these sensations—without judgment. Observe what you feel.
3. **Move Down Your Body:** Slowly move your attention downward, focusing on different parts of your body one at a time—your forehead, face, neck, shoulders, arms, chest, stomach, hips, legs, and feet. Take your time with each area, noticing how each part feels, and allow yourself to relax deeper.
4. **Breathe Into Tension:** If you encounter areas of tension or discomfort, take a deep breath and imagine sending your breath to that area. As you exhale, visualize releasing any tension from your body.
5. **Stay Present:** If your mind starts to wander, gently bring your focus back to the sensations in your body. Remember, this exercise is about noticing, not fixing or analyzing.
6. **Complete the Scan:** Once you've scanned your entire body, take a moment to notice how you feel overall. You may feel more relaxed, aware, or connected to your body.
7. **Repeat as Needed:** Practice this body scan daily or whenever you feel disconnected from your body. Regular use of this technique can enhance your ability to manage stress and anxiety.

# Worksheet: Body Scanning Techniques

- **Objective:** Use this worksheet to guide and track your practice of body scanning. This mindfulness exercise helps you connect with your body, identify areas of tension, and promote relaxation and stress relief.
- **Benefits:** Enhances bodily awareness, reduces anxiety, and provides a grounding tool to manage stress effectively.

## Step-by-Step Guide

### 1. Find a Comfortable Position

| | |
|---|---|
| Where did you practice this body scan (e.g., bed, chair, yoga mat)? | |
| Describe your position (e.g., sitting, lying down) | |
| Optional: Rate your stress or anxiety level before starting on a scale of 1-10 | |

## 2. Start at the Top of Your Head

Describe any sensations you noticed in your head or face (e.g., tightness in your forehead, relaxation in your jaw):

## 3. Move Down Your Body

For each body part, note any sensations you observed

| | |
|---|---|
| Neck | |
| Shoulders | |
| Arms | |
| Chest | |
| Stomach | |
| Hips | |
| Legs | |
| Feet | |

# 4. Breathe Into Tension

**Did you notice any areas of tension or discomfort?**

Yes

No

| Describe these areas and what they felt like (e.g., tight shoulders, heavy chest) | |
| How did breathing into those areas affect the sensations? | |

# 5. Stay Present

**Did your mind wander during the scan?**

Yes

No

| If so, how did you bring your focus back to your body? | |

# 6. Complete the Scan

How did you feel overall after completing the body scan (e.g., more relaxed, aware, or connected)?

Optional: Rate your stress or anxiety level after the exercise on a scale of 1-10

# Daily Practice Log

Date: _____     Time of Day: _____

Duration: _____

**What sensations or emotions did you notice during the scan?**

**Stress or anxiety level before and after practice (1-10)**

| Before | After |
|--------|-------|
|        |       |

**Additional Notes**

.......................................................................................................................................

.......................................................................................................................................

.......................................................................................................................................

.......................................................................................................................................

.......................................................................................................................................

.......................................................................................................................................

# Reflection Questions

What body part held the most tension today? How did focusing on it feel?

Which part of the scan felt the most relaxing or grounding? Why?

Did breathing into areas of tension help reduce discomfort? How?

How can you incorporate body scanning into your daily routine (e.g., before bed, during breaks)?

# Adapting Your Practice

## Quick 5-Minute Body Scan

**Which areas of your body will you focus on for a shorter scan?**

**How can this shorter version help during busy or stressful moments?**

## Extended 30-Minute Body Scan

**How can you create a relaxing environment for a deeper practice? (e.g., dim lights, soothing music):**

**How does the extended practice compare to the shorter version in terms of relaxation or awareness?**

# Weekly Self-Assessment

**How many times did you practice body scanning this week?**

**What changes have you noticed in your ability to manage stress or connect with your body?**

**What adjustments can you make to improve your practice (e.g., time of day, environment)?**

**What is your goal for next week's practice?**

# RELAX, RELEASE, RECHARGE: YOUR GUIDE TO PMR

Stress has a cunning way of getting into our bodies. Maybe you've felt it as a knot in your stomach before a big presentation or as a stiff neck after a long multitasking day. These tiny areas of stress can eventually wear us down on the inside as much as the outside. The good news? You don't have to carry that tension with you. Progressive muscle relaxation, or PMR, can help you relax one muscle at a time.

PMR is similar to a mild physical and mental workout; instead of growing muscle, you're learning how to let go of tension. The idea is simple: concentrate on one muscle group at a time, contracting it as you breathe in and relaxing it as you breathe out. In addition to promoting physical relaxation, this technique teaches your brain to identify how tension feels, making it easier for you to let it go in day-to-day situations.

Imagine this: You're finally relaxing in your favorite chair at the end of a long day. Starting with your feet, you curl your toes tightly, then slowly release them. Your body will feel lighter and more relaxed as you work up to your arms, legs, etc. When you're finished, you feel like you've released the day's tension, renewed and invigorated.

However, PMR is more than just relaxation; it's also about making room for calm and clarity. This technique is a useful addition to your self-care toolbox, whether you're using it to wind down before bed, prepare for a major meeting, or take a moment for yourself during a hectic day.

So, let's get started. This is your opportunity to pause, focus, and re-center your body and mind. You'll get closer to a profoundly relaxed and balanced state with each breath, squeeze, and release.

# Progressive Muscle Relaxation (PMR)

1. **Find a Quiet, Comfortable Space:** Find a quiet place where you won't be disturbed for your PMR session. Sit or lie down in a relaxed position.

2. **Center Yourself with Deep Breaths:** Take a few slow, deep breaths to center yourself and focus your mind. Inhale through your nose for a count of four, hold for two, and exhale through your mouth for a count of six.

3. **Start with Your Feet:** Begin with your feet. Tense the muscles in your toes for 5-10 seconds, then slowly release the tension. Focus on the sensation of relaxation that follows.

4. **Work Your Way Up:** Gradually move up your body, focusing on one muscle group at a time. Tense and relax the following areas:
   - Calves
   - Thighs
   - Abdomen
   - Chest
   - Hands
   - Arms
   - Shoulders
   - Neck
   - Face and Head

5. As you tense each muscle group, hold the tension for 5-10 seconds before releasing. Pay close attention to the contrast between the tension and the relaxation.

6. **Focus on Sensations of Relaxation:** After releasing tension from each muscle group, concentrate on the feeling of relaxation. Notice how the muscles soften and the stress dissipates from your body.

7. **Adjust for Shorter Sessions:** A quick 5-10 minute PMR session can relieve immediate stress if you're short on time. Focus on key areas of tension, such as your shoulders, neck, and jaw. Use the same tensing and relaxing technique to achieve a quick but effective release.

8. **Repeat as Needed:** Practice PMR regularly to improve your ability to manage tension and stress. You can perform an entire 30-minute session when time permits or use a shorter version for quick relief during moments of anxiety.

# Worksheet: Progressive Muscle Relaxation (PMR)

**Objective:** Use this worksheet to guide and track your PMR practice. This exercise helps reduce stress and tension by alternately tensing and relaxing muscle groups, promoting physical and emotional relaxation.

**Benefits:** Enhances body awareness, provides immediate stress relief, and fosters long-term tension management.

## STEP-BY-STEP GUIDE

### Find a Quiet, Comfortable Space

| Where did you practice PMR (e.g., bedroom, office, outdoor area)? | Describe your position (e.g., sitting, lying down): |
|---|---|
| | |

### Start with Your Feet

Describe the sensation after tensing and releasing your toes

# Work Your Way Up

Note the sensations you observed while tensing and releasing each muscle group:

| | |
|---|---|
| Calves | |
| Thighs | |
| Abdomen | |
| Chest | |
| Hands | |
| Arms | |
| Shoulders | |
| Neck | |
| Face and Head | |

## Center Yourself with Deep Breaths

| How did you feel after centering yourself with deep breaths (e.g., calm, focused)? | Optional: Rate your stress or tension level before starting on a scale of 1-10 |
|---|---|
| | |

# Focus on Sensations of Relaxation

**What did you notice about the contrast between tension and relaxation?**

**Did focusing on the sensations help reduce stress? How?**

# Adjust for Shorter Sessions

**Which key areas did you focus on for a quick session (e.g., shoulders, neck, jaw)?**

**How effective was the shorter session in relieving tension?**

**How long did you practice PMR today?**

**Optional: Rate your stress or tension level after the exercise on a scale of 1-10**

# DAILY PRACTICE LOG

**Date:** _____     **Time of Day:** _____

**Duration:** _____

| Which muscle groups felt the most tension today? | What sensations or emotions did you notice during practice? |
| --- | --- |
|  |  |

### Stress or tension level before and after practice (1-10)

| Before | After |
| --- | --- |
|  |  |

### Additional Notes

................................................................................

................................................................................

................................................................................

................................................................................

................................................................................

................................................................................

# REFLECTION QUESTIONS

Which muscle group felt the most relief today? Why?

Did you encounter any challenges while tensing or relaxing muscles (e.g., difficulty holding tension)?

How did focusing on the contrast between tension and relaxation affect your emotional state?

How can you integrate PMR into your daily routine (e.g., before bed, during work breaks)?

# ADAPTING YOUR PRACTICE

## Quick PMR Session (5-10 minutes)

Which key muscle groups will you focus on for shorter sessions?

How can this quicker version help during moments of acute stress?

## Full PMR Session (30 minutes)

How did the extended session enhance your sense of relaxation or awareness?

What adjustments could make the extended practice more effective?

# WEEKLY SELF-ASSESSMENT

How many times did you practice PMR this week?

What changes have you noticed in your ability to manage stress or tension?

What adjustments can you make to improve your PMR practice (e.g., focusing on specific muscle groups)?

What is your goal for next week's practice?

# HEALING THROUGH BREATHING

**Take a deep breath.** Inhale deeply, fill your lungs, and gently release it. Doesn't it feel good? That is the power of your breath. Your breath is one of the most basic yet powerful tools you have for healing your body and soothing your mind, yet it is often overlooked.

When life becomes stressful, it's easy to start breathing quickly and shallowly without realizing it. This type of breathing exacerbates feelings of stress and anxiety by telling your body that it is in "fight or flight" mode. However, you can change that with intention. By engaging in mindful breathing exercises, you can gradually guide your body out of stress mode and into a healing and relaxing state.

Imagine a time when everything seems too much, such as a hectic schedule, a conflict with a loved one, or an intense feeling of exhaustion. Imagine stopping, closing your eyes, and inhaling deeply and slowly. You hold it for a second, then let out the breath completely. Amidst the commotion, you have established a small, calm area.

Breathing exercises can be used for purposes other than calming you down. They can help you process challenging emotions, reestablish a connection with your body, and even sharpen your focus. Deep belly breathing, for example, tells your nervous system that it's acceptable to relax. A basic rhythmic breathing pattern can help calm a rushing mind, while alternate nostril breathing can help you balance your energies. This exercise aims to lead you through techniques that use your breath's inherent rhythm to support balance and healing. Consider it a way to press the reset button for your entire being, not just your body.

So, as we begin these exercises, remember that your breath is always there to help you reach a more peaceful, clear, and contented state. Your next breath can be the first step toward healing; it doesn't have to be complicated.

# DIAPHRAGMATIC BREATHING (DEEP BELLY BREATHING)

**Purpose:** Diaphragmatic breathing, also known as deep belly breathing, engages the diaphragm and encourages full oxygen exchange, helping to calm the nervous system and reduce stress.

- **Find a Comfortable Position:** Sit or lie down in a position that allows your hands to rest comfortably on your abdomen.
- **Take a Deep Breath In:** Slowly inhale through your nose for a count of four. Focus on expanding your diaphragm; your stomach should rise, but your chest should remain still.
- **Hold the Breath:** Hold the breath for a count of two, allowing the oxygen to circulate.
- **Exhale Slowly:** Exhale slowly through your mouth for a count of six. Feel your abdomen gently fall as the air leaves your body.
- **Repeat** this process for 5-10 breaths or until you feel more relaxed and centered.

# BOX BREATHING (4-4-4-4 METHOD)

**Purpose:** Box breathing is a structured breathing technique that helps calm the mind and body by promoting mindfulness and slowing the breath.

- **Find a Quiet Space:** Sit or stand in a quiet, comfortable place where you won't be interrupted.
- **Inhale for 4 Counts:** Inhale slowly through your nose for a count of four, focusing on filling your lungs.
- **Hold for 4 Counts:** Hold your breath for another four counts, feeling the stillness.
- **Exhale for 4 Counts:** Slowly exhale through your mouth for four counts, emptying your lungs.
- **Hold for 4 Counts Again:** Hold your breath again for a final count of four before starting the next cycle.
- **Repeat:** Continue this process for at least five cycles or until you feel a sense of calm.

Hold for 4

Breathe in for 4

Breathe out for 4

Start here

Hold for 4

# 4-7-8 BREATHING

**Purpose:** 4-7-8 breathing This helps calm the mind and body by using extended exhales to promote deep relaxation.

- **Get Comfortable:** Sit or lie down in a comfortable position with your hands resting on your abdomen.
- **Inhale for 4 Counts:** Breathe in slowly through your nose for a count of four, filling your lungs completely.
- **Hold for 7 Counts:** Hold your breath for a count of seven, keeping your body relaxed.
- **Exhale for 8 Counts:** Slowly exhale through your mouth for a count of eight, letting go of all the air in your lungs.
- **Repeat:** Continue this pattern for 4-5 cycles or until you feel more relaxed.

# PURSED LIP BREATHING

**Purpose:** Pursed Lip Breathing helps slow your breathing rate, easing tension and stress.

- **Sit in a Comfortable Position:** Relax your shoulders and neck and sit in a comfortable position.
- **Inhale Through Your Nose:** Inhale through your nose for two counts, keeping your mouth closed.
- **Purse Your Lips:** Pucker your lips like you're about to whistle.
- **Exhale Slowly:** Exhale slowly through your pursed lips for a count of four, letting out all the air in your lungs.
- **Repeat:** Continue this process for 5-10 breaths or until you feel a stress reduction.

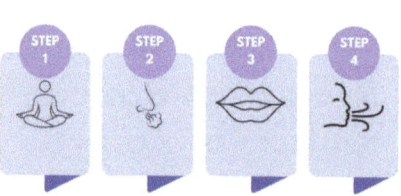

# ALTERNATE NOSTRIL BREATHING

**Purpose:** Alternate Nostril Breathing helps balance the nervous system and reduces stress by alternating breath through each nostril.

1. **Find a Relaxed Position:** Sit comfortably with your spine straight.
2. **Close Your Right Nostril:** Use your right thumb to close off your right nostril.
3. **Inhale Through the Left Nostril:** Slowly inhale through your left nostril for a count of four.
4. **Switch Nostrils:** Close your left nostril with your right ring finger and release your right nostril.
5. **Exhale Through the Right Nostril:** Exhale through the right nostril for a count of four.
6. **Inhale Through the Right Nostril:** Inhale through your right nostril for a count of four, then switch again, closing the right nostril and opening the left.
7. **Exhale Through the Left Nostril:** Exhale through your left nostril for a count of four.
8. **Repeat:** Continue alternating nostrils for 5-10 cycles.

# WORKSHEET: COMPREHENSIVE BREATHING EXERCISES

This worksheet guides you through five powerful breathing techniques—Diaphragmatic Breathing, Box Breathing, 4-7-8 Breathing, Alternate Nostril Breathing, and Pursed Lip Breathing. Each technique is designed to help you manage stress, calm your nervous system, and reconnect with the present moment.

## STEP 1: CHOOSE YOUR BREATHING TECHNIQUE

Select one or more breathing techniques to practice today.

- [ ] Pursed Lip Breathing
- [ ] 4-7-8 Breathing
- [ ] Box Breathing (4-4-4-4 Method)
- [ ] Alternate Nostril Breathing
- [ ] Diaphragmatic Breathing (Deep Belly Breathing)

# STEP 2: FOLLOW THE INSTRUCTIONS

## Diaphragmatic Breathing

**Position:** Sit or lie down comfortably, hands on your abdomen.

**Inhale:** Slowly breathe in through your nose for 4 counts, expanding your stomach.

**Hold:** Hold the breath for 2 counts.

**Exhale:** Exhale through your mouth for 6 counts, feeling your stomach fall.

**Repeat:** 5-10 breaths.

### What did you notice during this practice?

## Box Breathing (4-4-4-4)

**Position:** Find a quiet space.

**Inhale:** Breathe in through your nose for 4 counts.

**Hold:** Hold your breath for 4 counts.

**Exhale:** Exhale through your mouth for 4 counts.

**Hold Again:** Hold your breath for 4 counts.

**Repeat:** 5 cycles.

### How did this exercise affect your focus or stress levels?

## 4-7-8 breathing

**Position:** Sit or lie down comfortably.

**Inhale:** Slowly breathe in through your nose for 4 counts.

**Hold:** Hold your breath for 7 counts.

**Exhale:** Exhale through your mouth for 8 counts.

**Repeat:** 4-5 cycles.

### What changes did you feel in your body or mind?

## Pursed Lip Breathing

**Position:** Sit comfortably, relaxing your shoulders.

**Inhale:** Inhale through your nose for 2 counts.

**Purse Lips:** Pucker your lips as if whistling.

**Exhale:** Exhale slowly through pursed lips for 4 counts.

**Repeat:** 5-10 breaths.

### Did this technique help slow your breathing or ease tension?

## Alternate Nostril Breathing

**Position:** Sit comfortably with a straight spine.

**Close Right Nostril:** Use your thumb to close your right nostril.

**Inhale Left:** Inhale through your left nostril for 4 counts.

**Switch Nostrils:** Close your left nostril with your ring finger, and release your right nostril.

**Exhale Right:** Exhale through your right nostril for 4 counts.

**Inhale Right: Inhale through your right nostril for 4 counts.**

**Exhale Left: Exhale through your left nostril for 4 counts.**

**Repeat: 5-10 cycles.**

### How balanced or calm did you feel after this practice?

# STEP 3: REFLECT ON YOUR PRACTICE

### Which technique(s) felt most effective today?

### Did you notice any immediate changes in your mood or physical sensations?

### How long did you practice in total?

# STEP 4: PLAN FOR NEXT TIME

Frequency: How often will you practice these techniques? (e.g., daily, during stressful moments).

Goals: What benefits are you hoping to achieve with regular practice? (e.g., reduced anxiety, better focus).

## PRACTICE LOG

| Date | Techniques Used | Duration of Practice | Observations/Notes |
|------|-----------------|----------------------|--------------------|
|      |                 |                      |                    |
|      |                 |                      |                    |

## ADDITIONAL TIPS

- Combine techniques for a tailored practice. For example, start with Diaphragmatic Breathing and transition to 4-7-8 Breathing for deep relaxation.
- Use these techniques regularly, even during calm moments, to build resilience and control over your stress response.

# GENTLE YOGA POSES FOR EMOTIONAL HARMONY

Life can feel like an emotional rollercoaster. You can be at ease one minute and then suddenly feel overwhelmed, depressed, or frustrated. Even though emotions are a normal aspect of being human, they can occasionally throw us off balance. Imagine being able to gently lead yourself back to emotional balance. This is where yoga comes in—not just as a physical activity but also as a means of calming the spirit and mind.

Gentle yoga poses are like a conversation between your body and emotions. They facilitate stress relief, energy grounding, and the creation of an accepting environment for your emotions. These poses, whether a simple forward fold to relax your mind or a gentle twist to relieve stress, are subtle yet effective ways to help you discover your inner peace.

Imagine You're carrying the burden of your difficult day in your jaw, chest, or shoulders. Take a deep breath, sit comfortably, and unroll your yoga mat. As you move into a child's pose, your body softens, and your mind calms. After a short while, you're in a seated twist, and the mild stretch relieves stress you weren't even aware you were carrying. By the time you're done, you've regained your sense of calm, and your emotions are lighter.

Yoga is about establishing a safe space to breathe, move, and be; it's not about flexibility or flawless positions. No matter how you feel, these soft movements are made to meet you right where you are. Regular practice lets you see how these easy poses can help you process your emotions, manage stress, and regain your inner balance.

So roll out your mat (or locate a peaceful area), inhale deeply, and let's work through these easy yoga poses. With every step, you'll get closer to finding inner peace.

# SOMATIC YOGA POSES

**Purpose:** Gentle yoga poses are a powerful tool to release physical tension and promote emotional balance. These simple poses, such as Child's Pose and Cat-Cow, help you connect with your body and calm your mind. Regularly practicing these poses can help you reduce stress, enhance mindfulness, and restore balance to your nervous system.

## CHILD'S POSE TRANSITION INTO CAT-COW

**1. Find a Quiet, Comfortable Space:** Find a comfortable space to practice undisturbed. Use a yoga mat or a soft surface to support your knees and hands.

**2. Start with Child's Pose (Balasana):**

- Kneel on the Floor: Kneel, bringing your big toes together and sitting back on your heels.
- Extend Your Arms: Stretch your arms forward, palms facing the mat, and slowly lower your forehead to the ground.
- Relax Into the Pose: Let your shoulders relax, and your chest melts toward the floor. Breathe deeply, focusing on the sensation of release in your back, hips, and shoulders.
- Hold for 5-10 Breaths: Stay in this pose for 5-10 deep breaths, using each exhale to deepen your relaxation.

**3. Transition to Cat-Cow (Marjaryasana-Bitilasana):**

- Get on Hands and Knees: Come onto all fours, placing your hands directly under your shoulders and your knees under your hips. Spread your fingers wide to create a stable base.
- Move Into Cow Pose (Bitilasana): Inhale as you arch your back. Lift your chest, head toward the ceiling, and gently raise your tailbone. Feel the stretch along your spine and front body.
- Move Into Cat Pose (Marjaryasana): Exhale as you round your back. Tuck your chin toward your chest and draw your tailbone inward, creating a gentle stretch along the back body.
- Repeat for 5-10 Rounds: Continue moving between Cat and Cow poses, following your breath. Inhale as you arch (Cow), and exhale as you round (Cat). Allow the movement to be slow and intentional, focusing on how your body feels in each position.

**4. Focus on Your Breath:** Connect your movement to your breath with each pose. Inhale deeply through your nose and exhale slowly through your mouth. This mindful breathing helps activate the parasympathetic nervous system, promoting relaxation and calming the mind.

**5. Practice for Less Than 30 Minutes a Day:** These poses can be done in under 30 minutes, making them a perfect addition to your daily routine. If you have limited time, focus on holding each pose for a few minutes, letting the benefits accumulate over time.

**6. Repeat as Needed:** Integrate these poses into your day whenever you feel tension or stress building. With regular practice, Child's Pose and Cat-Cow can help you maintain emotional balance and stay grounded throughout the day.

## ADDITIONAL RECOMMENDATIONS

- **Savasana (Corpse Pose):** After completing your session, lie flat on your back in Savasana for a few minutes. This pose allows you to integrate the benefits of your practice and find complete relaxation.

- **Modify if Needed:** Use a blanket under your knees or forehead for extra support in the Child's Pose if needed, or take breaks if the movement feels too intense.

Cow

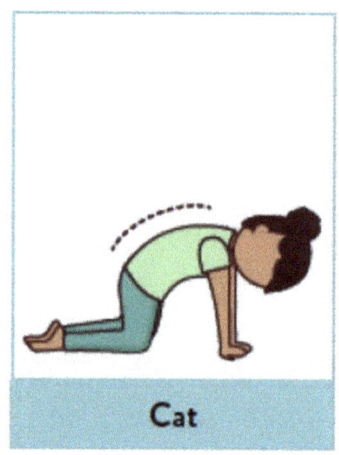
Cat

# TAI CHI TRANQUILITY

**Purpose:** Tai Chi is a gentle practice integrating mindful movement and deep breathing to enhance emotional well-being and reduce anxiety. The slow, flowing movements help you stay grounded and connected to your body while calming the mind. One effective sequence to begin with is "Wave Hands Like Clouds," which promotes balance, relaxation, and mindfulness.

**1. Find a Quiet, Open Space:** Choose a space where you have room to move comfortably. Ideally, practice Tai Chi in a peaceful environment, such as a quiet room or outside in nature.

**2. Begin in a Standing Position:**

- Stand with Your Feet Shoulder-Width Apart: Align your feet parallel, about hip- or shoulder-width apart.
- Soften Your Knees: Slightly bend your knees to release tension and create a stable, relaxed stance. Keep your back straight but not rigid.

**3. Shift Your Weight:**

- Shift to One Foot: As you inhale, gently shift your weight to your right foot, feeling grounded and stable.
- Move with Awareness: Slowly shift your weight to your left foot as you exhale. Allow your movements to be slow and controlled, fully feeling the transfer of balance from one side to the other.

**4. "Wave Hands Like Clouds" Sequence:**

- Hand Movement: While shifting your weight, begin to move your hands in a gentle, waving motion. Imagine your hands floating like clouds. Keep your movements fluid and soft.
- Coordinate with Your Breath: Inhale as your hands rise gently and move to one side, and exhale as they lower and shift to the other side. Allow your breath to guide the movement.
- Focus on the Flow: Continue this pattern, feeling a continuous flow of energy through your body as you shift your weight and wave your hands.

## 5. Mindful Breathing:

- Inhale deeply through your nose and exhale slowly through your mouth, allowing your breath to sync with the movement. This focused breathing helps calm the nervous system, reduces stress, and promotes relaxation.

## 6. Practice for 5-10 Minutes or More:

- Continue the "Wave Hands Like Clouds" sequence for 5-10 minutes or up to 30 minutes for a full session. As you practice, focus on your body and breath, allowing anxious thoughts to melt away with each movement.

## 7. Repeat Daily for Emotional Well-Being:

- Incorporate this practice into your daily routine to experience long-term benefits. Even practicing Tai Chi for just 30 minutes a day can significantly enhance your emotional balance, mindfulness, and overall well-being.

## ADDITIONAL RECOMMENDATIONS

- **Adjust for Comfort:** Adjust your stance or slow the movement even further if you feel any tension or discomfort. Tai Chi is meant to be gentle and calming, so modify it to suit your needs.

- **End with Stillness:** After completing your Tai Chi sequence, take a moment to stand still with your hands by your sides. Close your eyes, breathe deeply, and feel the calm the practice has brought to your body and mind.

# DANCING YOUR WAY TO EMOTIONAL BALANCE AND RELEASE

**Purpose:** Dance and free movement are powerful tools for emotional expression and regulation. By moving intuitively to your favorite music, you can connect with your emotions and release tension stored in your body. This practice promotes both immediate relief and long-term emotional balance.

**1. Find a Comfortable, Open Space:** Choose a space where you can move freely without restriction. It can be in a room, outside, or anywhere you feel comfortable to express yourself through movement.

**2. Select Music that Resonates with You:** Pick music that suits your mood or emotions. It could be calming, energizing, or something that helps you express feelings you need to process. Let the music guide your movement.

**3. Start with Gentle Movements:**

- Begin Slowly: Start by standing with your feet slightly apart. Allow your body to relax, and take a few deep breaths to center yourself.
- Tune into Your Body: Begin by gently swaying or shifting your weight from one foot to the other. Let your body warm up as you gradually ease into the movement.

**4. Allow Your Movement to Evolve:**

- Intuitive Movement: As the music progresses, let your body move in any way that feels right. Whether swaying, twirling, or energetic dancing, focus on how your body naturally responds to the rhythm and beats.
- Express Your Emotions: Your movements might be slow and fluid if you feel calm. Your movements become more energetic or vigorous if you process more intense emotions. Let your body express what words can't.

**5. Stay Present and Focus on Breath:**

- Throughout your movement, remain mindful of your breathing. Take deep breaths as you move, allowing your breath's rhythm to sync with your body's flow. This keeps you grounded and helps you stay in the present moment.

## 6. Release Tension and Emotions:

- Allow yourself to release any tension or stored emotions during your dance. Whether you're moving energetically or calmly, the process of physical expression helps release emotional and physical stress.

## 7. Dance for 20-30 Minutes:

- Move intuitively for 20-30 minutes, using this time to fully explore the range of motion and expression your body needs. You may change the music to reflect different emotions or stay with one mood throughout the session.

8. **Repeat Regularly for Emotional Regulation:** Incorporate dance or free movement into your routine whenever you feel emotionally overwhelmed or disconnected from your body. Regular practice will help improve your emotional balance and self-awareness over time.

## ADDITIONAL RECOMMENDATIONS

- **End with Stillness or Stretching:** After your dance session, take a moment to stand still and breathe, allowing your body to settle. You can also incorporate gentle stretching to cool down.

- **Use Movement to Address Specific Emotions:** Focus on slow, grounding movements if you feel anxious. If you're sad or angry, more energetic, fast-paced movements may help release those emotions.

# WORKSHEET: GENTLE MOVEMENT PRACTICES

**Objective**: Explore and practice gentle movement techniques, yoga poses, Tai Chi, and free movement dance to release physical tension, process emotions, and promote emotional balance.

**Benefits**: Combines mindfulness, physical movement, and emotional expression to reduce stress, enhance self-awareness, and improve overall well-being.

## STEP-BY-STEP GUIDE FOR MOVEMENT PRACTICES

### Calm Within: Gentle Yoga Poses

**Purpose**: Use simple poses like Child's Pose and Cat-Cow to connect with your body and calm your mind.

| Find a Quiet Space: Where are you practicing? (e.g., living room, park, studio) |
| --- |
| |

### Child's Pose (Balasana)

| How did it feel to stretch your arms forward and let your chest melt toward the floor? | How many breaths did you take while holding the pose? |
| --- | --- |
| | |

### Cat-Cow (Marjaryasana-Bitilasana)

| What sensations did you notice as you moved between Cat and Cow poses (e.g., spine stretch, relaxation)? | Did coordinating your movement with your breath enhance the relaxation? Yes / No |
| --- | --- |
| | |

# TAI CHI TRANQUILITY: "WAVE HANDS LIKE CLOUDS"

**Purpose:** Integrate slow, mindful movements with deep breathing to create calm and balance.

| Find an Open Space: Describe your space (e.g., outdoor patio, yoga studio) |
|---|
| |

| Begin in a Standing Position: Did aligning your feet and softening your knees create a sense of stability? Yes / No |
|---|
| |

## Wave Hands Like Clouds Sequence

| How did your body feel as you shifted weight and waved your hands? (e.g., balanced, relaxed) | Did syncing your breath with the movement help you stay grounded? Yes / No |
|---|---|
| | |

| Duration: How long did you practice this sequence? |
|---|
| |

# FLOW FREELY: DANCING FOR EMOTIONAL BALANCE

**Purpose:** Use intuitive dance to release tension and connect with your emotions.

| Select Music: What music did you choose? (e.g., calming, energetic) | Begin with Gentle Movements: How did it feel to sway or shift your weight? (e.g., relaxed, hesitant) |
|---|---|
| | |

## Allow Movement to Evolve

| What emotions or sensations did you express through your movement? | Was the movement slow and fluid, or energetic and vigorous? |
|---|---|
| | |

**Stay Present and Focus on Breath:** Did syncing your breath with your movements help you stay mindful?
Yes / No

# DAILY PRACTICE LOG

| | |
|---|---|
| **Date & Time of Day** | |
| **Duration** | |
| **Post-Exercise Heart Rate Variability** | |
| **Initial Heart Rate Variability** | |
| **Which practice(s) did you complete? (Check all that apply).** | ☐ Child's Pose<br><br>☐ Cat-Cow<br><br>☐ Tai Chi<br><br>☐ Wave Hands Like Clouds Sequence<br><br>☐ Flow Freely Dancing |
| **Additional Notes** | |

# SOOTHING THE SENSES: SUPPORT FOR MENTAL HEALTH

When life becomes overwhelming, it sometimes seems like the world is too bright, too noisy, or simply too much. Stress and trauma have a way of intensifying everything, trapping you in a cycle of anxiety and tension. But what if you could focus on your senses to obtain peace and comfort? This exercise aims to use your senses to create healing, grounding, and relief moments.

You can return to the present moment by using your senses—sight, hearing, smell, touch, and taste—as anchors. When your thoughts are racing or your emotions feel overwhelming, using your senses can gently remind you that you are safe and present. For instance, the fragrance of lavender, the sound of rain, or the feel of a cozy blanket can evoke a sense of peace that words can't always express.

Think of a time when you felt stressed or anxious. Perhaps you reached for a warm cup of tea out of habit, turned on calming music, or went outside to enjoy the fresh air. Even though those small acts might have seemed insignificant at the time, they were your senses helping you find balance. Now imagine consciously using these resources to promote your mental well-being, even in the most trying circumstances.

These exercises teach you how to use your senses to help you feel less traumatized and more at ease. You will learn how sensory techniques, such as grounding visualizations, tactile objects, or aromatherapy, can help establish a safe zone in your body and mind. The best part? These procedures are easy to follow, available, and customizable to meet your needs.

You don't need to make significant, drastic changes before you heal. Sometimes, it's as easy as holding something soft, lighting a candle, or listening to a calming tune. These techniques are meant to remind you that healing is a process and that every little step counts.

# THE HEALING POWER OF AROMATHERAPY

**Purpose:** Aromatherapy uses essential oils to promote emotional and physical healing by engaging the sense of smell. It's a powerful tool in somatic therapy for reducing anxiety, alleviating stress, and supporting trauma recovery. The olfactory system is closely linked to the brain's emotional centers, meaning inhaling calming scents can quickly promote peace and relaxation. Specific essential oils can calm the nervous system, trigger relaxation responses, and help you reconnect with your body.

**1. Choose Your Essential Oils:** Select essential oils that target your specific needs. Some effective oils for anxiety, stress, and trauma include:

- Lavender: Promotes relaxation and reduces anxiety.
- Chamomile: Calms nerves and eases tension.
- Frankincense: Helps alleviate feelings of stress and trauma.
- Ylang-Ylang: Balances emotions and promotes a sense of peace.
- Bergamot: Uplifts the mood and reduces stress.
- Rose: Provides comfort and emotional healing.

**2. Decide on Your Application Method:** There are several ways to incorporate aromatherapy into your practice:

- Diffusion: An essential oil diffuser releases calming scents into the air.
- Topical Application: Dilute essential oils with carrier oil (like coconut or jojoba oil) and apply them to pulse points (wrists, neck, temples).
- Inhalation: Place a few drops on a handkerchief or inhale directly from the bottle for quick relief.
- Bath Soak: Add a few drops of essential oil to a warm bath to create a relaxing, immersive experience.

**3. Set the Mood:** Before beginning your aromatherapy session, find a quiet, comfortable space to sit or lie down undisturbed. Dim the lights, put on soothing music, and allow yourself to fully relax in the environment.

## 4. Start with Deep Breathing:

- Inhale the Aroma: If using a diffuser, sit comfortably and close your eyes. Inhale deeply, taking in the calming scent of the essential oils. If applying topically, gently rub your wrists or neck and breathe in the aroma. Please focus on the scent and allow it to ground you in the present moment.

- Exhale Slowly: As you exhale, imagine releasing any tension or anxiety in your body. Repeat this for 5-10 deep breaths.

## 5. Use a Guided Sensory Meditation (Optional): For added benefit, guide yourself through a sensory meditation while inhaling the essential oils:

- Focus on the Scent: What memories or emotions does the scent evoke? Allow your mind to explore any thoughts that arise without judgment.

- Stay Present: Focus on how your body feels as you breathe deeply. The scent serves as an anchor, helping you stay connected to your body and reducing anxious or distressing thoughts.

## 6. Continue for 10-20 Minutes: Remain in this state of deep breathing and sensory engagement for 10-20 minutes, or longer if time allows. Let the aroma ease your nervous system and release stored emotional tension.

## 7. Incorporate Aromatherapy into Your Daily Routine: Aromatherapy can be used throughout the day as part of your daily routine for ongoing stress relief. Diffuse oils in your home or workspace, apply them during moments of high stress, or use them before bed to improve sleep and relaxation.

# ADDITIONAL RECOMMENDATIONS

**Rotate Oils for Different Effects:** Try different essential oils based on your emotional needs. Use lavender or chamomile to calm anxiety before sleep or bergamot and ylang-ylang to uplift your mood during the day.

**Ensure Proper Dilution:** Always dilute oils with a carrier oil to prevent skin irritation when applying oils topically. A good ratio is 2-3 drops of essential oil per teaspoon of carrier oil.

# WORKSHEET: AROMATHERAPY FOR ANXIETY AND EMOTIONAL BALANCE

**Objective**: Use this worksheet to guide your practice of aromatherapy, helping you reduce anxiety, alleviate stress, and support emotional healing.

**Benefits**: Aromatherapy engages the sense of smell to calm the nervous system, trigger relaxation, and promote mindfulness and self-connection.

**Purpose**: Use this worksheet to guide your practice of aromatherapy. Engage your sense of smell to reduce anxiety, alleviate stress, and support emotional healing. Aromatherapy is a powerful tool for calming the nervous system and reconnecting with the present moment.

## STEP 1: CHOOSE YOUR ESSENTIAL OILS

Step 1: Which essential oil(s) did you select for this session?

- [ ] Lavender
- [ ] Bergamot
- [ ] Chamomile
- [ ] Rose
- [ ] Frankincense
- [ ] Ylang-Ylang
- [ ] Other:

Why did you choose these oils? (e.g., relaxation, emotional healing).

## STEP 2: DECIDE ON YOUR APPLICATION METHOD

Which application method(s) are you using today? (Check all that apply)

- [ ] Diffusion
- [ ] Topical Application
- [ ] Inhalation
- [ ] Bath Soak
- [ ] Other:

## Describe your setup

## STEP 3: SET THE MOOD

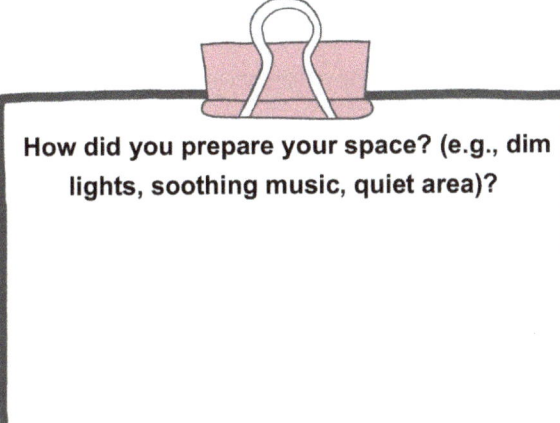

How did you prepare your space? (e.g., dim lights, soothing music, quiet area)?

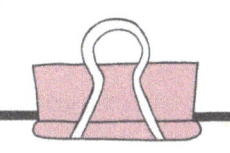

Describe your environment

## STEP 4: START WITH DEEP BREATHING

### Did you follow the deep breathing instructions?

Yes

No

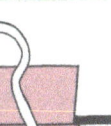

How many breaths did you take during this exercise?

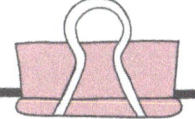

What sensations or changes did you notice during deep breathing? (e.g., relaxation, tension release, emotional responses)

# STEP 5: GUIDED SENSORY MEDITATION (OPTIONAL)

**Did you include a guided sensory meditation?**

Yes

No

If yes, what memories or emotions did the scent evoke?

How did the scent help anchor you in the present moment?

# STEP 6: CONTINUE FOR 10-20 MINUTES

How long did you spend in your aromatherapy session? (e.g., 10 minutes, 20 minutes)

Did you feel any physical or emotional changes after this session? (e.g., reduced stress, calmness, better focus)?

# STEP 7: INCORPORATE AROMATHERAPY INTO YOUR ROUTINE

How will you use aromatherapy in your daily life? (e.g., before bed, during stressful moments, while working).

Which oils or methods will you try next?

# REFLECTION AND NOTES

| What worked well in this session? | What would you change or improve for next time? | Additional Observations |
|---|---|---|
| | | |

# PRACTICE LOG

| Date | Essential Oil(s) Used | Application Method | Duration | Effects Noticed |
|---|---|---|---|---|
| | | | | |
| | | | | |

# ADDITIONAL TIPS

- Rotate oils to match your emotional needs throughout the day.
- Always dilute oils for topical use (2-3 drops per teaspoon of carrier oil).
- Experiment with different oils and methods to find your personal preferences.

Enjoy the healing power of scents and their ability to promote emotional balance and well-being!!!

# MUSIC THERAPY FOR EMOTIONAL BALANCE

## PURPOSE

Music therapy is a powerful sensory technique that can create emotional balance, reduce stress, and help process trauma. Music profoundly affects mood and emotions, making it a valuable tool in somatic therapy. Using music intentionally can soothe the nervous system, manage emotional responses, and foster healing.

**1. Choose Your Music:** Select music that resonates with your emotional state or the goal of your session. Here are some types of music to consider:

- Calming Music: Soft, instrumental, or natural sounds (e.g., rain, ocean waves) to promote relaxation.
- Uplifting Music: Melodic, cheerful tunes to lift your mood and provide emotional relief.
- Deep, Reflective Music: Classical or ambient music for introspective sessions aimed at processing emotions and trauma.

**2. Experiment with different genres to find what best suits your needs.**

**3. Set the Stage:** Create a comfortable environment to engage with the music fully. Sit or lie down in a quiet space, dim the lights if necessary, and ensure no distractions. This will help you focus solely on the therapeutic experience.

**4. Start with Deep Breathing:**

- Inhale Deeply: Before playing the music, take a few deep breaths to calm your mind and body. Inhale through your nose for a count of four, and exhale through your mouth for six.
- Let Go of Tension: With each exhale, consciously release any tension in your body. This will help prepare you to receive the calming effects of the music.

**5. Engage with the Music:**

- Press Play: Start your chosen playlist and close your eyes if that feels comfortable. Let the music wash over you, noticing how it affects your emotions and body.
- Focus on Your Breath: As you listen, breathe slowly and deeply. Let the rhythm and melody guide your breath and ground you in the present moment.

- Observe Emotional Reactions: Pay attention to how the music impacts your emotions. Do certain notes or instruments evoke specific feelings? Allow yourself to feel whatever emotions arise without judgment.

**6. Use Music to Process Trauma or Stress:**
- Reflect on Emotions: If you're processing trauma or stress, focus on how the music can help express or release those emotions. Let the music be a tool for emotional expression. For instance, faster tempos allow you to release pent-up energy, while slower, soothing sounds can help you calm down.
- Body Scan with Music: You can incorporate a body scan, noticing any tension in your body as you listen. Let the music guide your awareness to areas of tension, using its calming effects to help release tightness or stress.

**7. Play for 20-30 Minutes:** Engage with your music therapy session for at least 20-30 minutes, giving yourself ample time to relax into the experience. Whether you're processing trauma or simply looking to relieve stress, this time will allow the music to take full effect.

**8. Incorporate Music into Your Daily Routine:** Music therapy can be a powerful daily tool. Use calming music in the background while you work, play relaxing tunes before bed, or choose energizing songs in the morning to start your day with emotional balance. Over time, this practice can enhance your emotional regulation and overall well-being.

## ADDITIONAL RECOMMENDATIONS

**Vocalize if It Feels Right:** If you're moved to sing or hum along with the music, let yourself do so. Vocalizing can enhance emotional release and deepen the connection with the music.

**Change the Tempo to Match Your Needs:** Use slow, soothing music when you need calm and more upbeat, rhythmic tunes when you need to release energy or process difficult emotions.

# WORKSHEET: THE HEALING SOUNDTRACK

**Objective:** This worksheet guides your music therapy sessions, helping you use music to manage stress, regulate emotions, and process trauma. By engaging with music intentionally, you can tap into its power to soothe the nervous system, encourage emotional release, and promote healing.

**Benefits:**

- Reduces stress and anxiety
- Fosters mindfulness and emotional balance
- Enhances emotional healing and trauma processing

## STEP 1: CHOOSE YOUR MUSIC

What type of music did you select for this session? (Check all that apply)

- [ ] Calming Music (e.g., nature sounds)
- [ ] Deep, Reflective Music (e.g., classical
- [ ] Uplifting Music (e.g., cheerful)
- [ ] Other

| Why did you choose this type of music? (e.g., relaxation, emotional uplift, introspection) | What specific song(s), artist(s), or playlist(s) are you using? |
|---|---|
|  |  |

## STEP 2: SET THE STAGE

| Describe your environment | Is the space quiet and comfortable? (e.g., dimmed lights, no distractions) |
|---|---|
|  |  |

| What other steps did you take to create a relaxing atmosphere? (e.g., lighting candles, using a blanket) |
| --- |
| |

## STEP 3: START WITH DEEP BREATHING

**Did you begin with deep breathing?**

Yes

No

| How many breaths did you take before starting the music? (e.g., 3, 5, 10)? | Did the deep breathing help prepare you for the session? If so, how? |
| --- | --- |
| | |

## STEP 4: ENGAGE WITH THE MUSIC

| What sensations or emotions did you notice as you listened to the music? (e.g., relaxation,) | Did the rhythm or melody affect your breathing or heartbeat? How? | Did any particular notes, instruments, or lyrics evoke strong emotions? |
| --- | --- | --- |
| | | |

## STEP 5: USE MUSIC TO PROCESS TRAUMA OR STRESS

**Reflect on Emotions: Did the music help you express or release emotions?**

Yes

No

| If yes, describe how | Body Scan with Music: Did you notice any tension in your body? Where? |
|---|---|
|  |  |

**Were you able to release tension as you listened?**

Yes                No

## STEP 6: DURATION AND REFLECTION

| How long did you engage with the music therapy session? (e.g., 20 minutes, 30 minutes) |
|---|
|  |

| How did you feel before starting the session? (Rate 1-10: 1 = very stressed, 10 = completely calm) | How did you feel after completing the session? (Rate 1-10) |
|---|---|
|  |  |

## STEP 7: INCORPORATE MUSIC INTO YOUR DAILY ROUTINE

| How will you use music therapy in your daily life? (e.g., during work). | What types of music will you explore in future sessions? |
|---|---|
|  |  |

# REFLECTION AND NOTES

| What worked well in this session? | What would you do differently next time? | Additional Observations |
|---|---|---|
| | | |

# PRACTICE LOG

| Date | Music Selected | Duration of Session | Effects Noticed |
|---|---|---|---|
| | | | |
| | | | |

# ADDITIONAL TIPS

- Experiment with vocalizing if it feels natural; singing or humming can enhance emotional release.
- Adjust the tempo of the music to match your needs—slow for relaxation or upbeat for releasing energy.
- Regularly incorporate music into your life for ongoing emotional balance and well-being.

# TACTILE STIMULATION FOR EMOTIONAL BALANCE

**Purpose:** Tactile stimulation is a powerful sensory technique that helps ground you in the present moment by focusing on physical sensations. Whether you're holding a smooth stone, a piece of fabric, or a stress ball, the act of engaging with these objects can provide immediate relief from anxiety, trauma, or dissociation. This simple, practical method offers a tangible way to manage stress and promote long-term emotional regulation.

**1. Select Your Tactile Object:** Identify an object that brings you comfort or helps ground you. Some effective choices include:

- Smooth Stone: Its solid, cool texture can provide a calming effect.
- Piece of Fabric: Soft fabric or textured cloth can be soothing to the touch.
- Stress Ball: Squeezing a stress ball helps release tension and provides physical engagement.

**2.** Choose an object that resonates with you and can easily be carried throughout your day.

**3. Keep Your Object Accessible:** Carry your tactile object with you, especially if you anticipate stressful situations or moments of high anxiety. Place it in your pocket or bag or on your desk for quick access.

**4. Engage with the Object During Stressful Moments:**

- Hold the Object: When you feel anxious, overwhelmed, or dissociated, take the object in your hand.
- Focus on the Texture: Pay close attention to the object's texture, weight, and temperature. If it's a smooth stone, feel the cool surface and notice its shape. If it's fabric, focus on its softness or texture.
- Press or Squeeze: If using a stress ball, gently press or squeeze the ball in your hand, releasing muscle tension while keeping your mind focused on the sensation.

**5.** Stay Present with the Sensations:

- Stay Grounded: As you engage with the object, focus on how your body feels in the moment. This physical sensation helps bring your attention back to the present, interrupting any spiraling thoughts or anxiety.

- Breathe Deeply: Take slow, deep breaths as you engage with the tactile object. Inhale through your nose and exhale through your mouth, using the physical sensation to anchor your breath.

**6.** Use Tactile Stimulation During Anxiety or Dissociation: Tactile stimulation is particularly effective during moments of high anxiety or dissociation. Holding the object provides a tangible point of focus, helping you feel more connected to your body and the present moment.

**7.** Practice for Immediate Relief: Continue holding and focusing on the object for as long as needed. Most people experience relief after just a few minutes of tactile engagement. Still, you can continue as long as it feels helpful.

**8.** Incorporate Tactile Stimulation into Your Daily Routine: Integrate this technique into your daily life to manage stress. Whether you're in a meeting, commuting, or at home, holding your grounding object can help maintain a sense of calm and balance.

## ADDITIONAL RECOMMENDATIONS

**Experiment with Different Objects:** Try using various objects—smooth, rough, soft, or firm—until you find one that best suits your needs.

**Use Alongside Other Grounding Techniques:** Combine tactile stimulation with breathing exercises, sensory grounding, or movement techniques for a more comprehensive approach to managing stress and anxiety.

# WORKSHEET: TACTILE STIMULATION

**Objective:** Use this worksheet to guide and track your practice of tactile stimulation as a grounding technique. This method helps manage anxiety, trauma, and dissociation by focusing on physical sensations.

**Benefits:** Provides immediate relief from stress, enhances present-moment awareness, and supports long-term emotional regulation.

## STEP-BY-STEP GUIDE FOR TACTILE STIMULATION

What object did you choose? (Check all that apply)

- [ ] Smooth Stone
- [ ] Stress Ball
- [ ] Piece of Fabric
- [ ] Other

**Why did you select this object?**

## ENGAGE WITH THE OBJECT DURING STRESSFUL MOMENTS

| Hold the Object: How did the object feel in your hand (e.g., cool, soft, firm)? | Focus on the Texture: Describe the object's texture, weight, and temperature | Press or Squeeze: If using a stress ball, how did squeezing or pressing the object help release tension? |
|---|---|---|
| | | |

# KEEP YOUR OBJECT ACCESSIBLE

**Where do you keep your tactile object for quick access (e.g., pocket, desk, bag)?**

# STAY PRESENT WITH THE SENSATIONS

| **Grounding: How did focusing on the object's physical sensations affect your thoughts or emotions?** | **How many breaths did you take while engaging with the object?** |
| --- | --- |
| | |

**Did pairing tactile stimulation with deep breathing enhance your sense of calm?**

Yes

No

# USE TACTILE STIMULATION DURING ANXIETY OR DISSOCIATION

| **Describe the situation when you used tactile stimulation (e.g., feeling overwhelmed at work, experiencing dissociation at home)** | **How did the tactile object help you reconnect with your body and the present moment?** |
| --- | --- |
| | |

# PRACTICE FOR IMMEDIATE RELIEF

**How long did you engage with your tactile object today?**

**Did you notice a sense of relief or calm afterward?**

Yes [   ]     No [   ]

Rate your stress or anxiety level before and after the exercise on a scale of 1-10.

| Before | After |
|--------|-------|
|        |       |

# PRACTICE LOG

| Date | Time of Day | Object Used | Duration |
|------|-------------|-------------|----------|
|      |             |             |          |

**What sensations or emotions did you notice during practice?**

.................................................................................................................................

.................................................................................................................................

.................................................................................................................................

.................................................................................................................................

**Stress or anxiety level before and after practice (1-10)**

| Before | After |
|--------|-------|
|        |       |

# REFLECTION QUESTIONS

Which tactile object felt most effective today? Why?

Did tactile stimulation help you stay present and manage stress? How?

Did pairing this technique with deep breathing or other grounding exercises enhance its effectiveness?

How can you incorporate tactile stimulation into your daily routine?

103

# WEEKLY SELF-ASSESSMENT

### How many times did you use tactile stimulation this week?

### Which object or technique felt most grounding? Why?

### What changes did you notice in your ability to manage stress or anxiety?

### What adjustments will you make to improve your practice next week?

## Additional Recommendations

- Experiment with Different Objects: Try using a variety of objects to discover what feels most effective (e.g., smooth vs. rough, soft vs. firm).

- Combine Techniques: Pair tactile stimulation with breathing exercises, body scanning, or mindfulness for enhanced grounding and relaxation.

- Use Preventively: Engage with your tactile object during low-stress moments to strengthen the habit and make it easier to use during high-stress situations.

# VAGUS NERVE RESET: 30 MINUTES TO EMOTIONAL REGULATION

Have you ever wished you could turn on a switch to regulate your emotions and nerves and feel more grounded? The fact that your body has such a "switch" may surprise you. The vagus nerve is an amazing pathway that connects your brain to your lungs, heart, and digestive system. It influences your mood, stress levels, and general sense of well-being. By learning how to activate and reset your vagus nerve, you can achieve a higher degree of emotional regulation and inner tranquility.

The vagus nerve is central to the body's parasympathetic nervous system and is responsible for the "rest and digest" state. The vagus nerve can help you regain balance while you're in fight-or-flight mode due to stress, anxiety, or unresolved emotions. You can approach life with more peace and clarity by resetting it, like pressing a mental and emotional refresh button.

Think about a moment when you could not get rid of the "on edge" feeling and felt overburdened or agitated. Imagine spending only half an hour slowly guiding your mind and body out of that state. You could employ techniques like deep diaphragmatic breathing, humming, or even basic cold exposure, such as sprinkling icy water on your face. By activating the vagus nerve, these techniques let your body know it's okay to relax.

This exercise introduces you to various easily accessible techniques for resetting your vagus nerve. They are not difficult or time-consuming, but they are powerful. Each technique, which ranges from rhythmic breathing to specific movements, is intended to help you control your emotions, strengthen your ability to withstand stress, and reestablish your inner calm.

The best part? You always have these tools on hand, ready to go whenever needed. Whether you're beginning your day, ending it at night, or getting through a difficult time, you can take charge of your emotions—one step closer to emotional harmony. Together, we can reset your vagus nerve and help you uncover the balance and serenity within you during this 30-minute journey.

# DIAPHRAGMATIC BREATHING (BELLY BREATHING)

> **Purpose:** Diaphragmatic breathing promotes relaxation, reduces stress, and enhances vagal tone. It is an effective method for improving oxygen exchange and calming the nervous system. Practice this technique for 5-10 minutes daily to experience noticeable emotional regulation and overall well-being improvements.

1. **Find a Comfortable Position:** Sit or lie down in a relaxed position. You can do this exercise in bed, on the couch, or in a chair with your back supported.
2. **Place Your Hands:** Rest one hand on your chest and the other on your abdomen to help monitor your breathing.
3. **Inhale Deeply:** Breathe in through your nose, allowing your abdomen to rise while keeping your chest still. Focus on filling your lower lungs.
4. **Exhale Slowly:** Breathe through your mouth, feeling your abdomen fall as you release your breath.
5. **Repeat for 5-10 Minutes:** Continue this cycle for 5-10 minutes, focusing on slow, deep breaths.

# COHERENT BREATHING

> **Purpose:** Coherent breathing helps balance the autonomic nervous system, reduces anxiety, and increases heart rate variability (HRV). Maintaining a consistent breathing rate can quickly achieve a calm and focused state. Practice for 5-10 minutes a day.

1. **Get Comfortable:** Sit comfortably with your feet flat on the floor or lie down in a quiet space.
2. **Breathe In:** Inhale slowly through your nose for a count of 6.
3. **Breathe Out:** Exhale gently through your mouth for a count of 6.
4. **Establish Rhythm:** Continue breathing in and out, maintaining this rhythm of approximately 5 breaths per minute.
5. **Practice for 5-10 Minutes:** Aim to keep your breathing rate consistent for the entire practice.

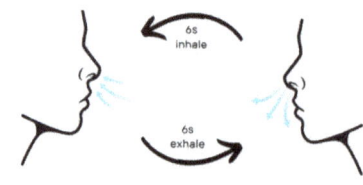

# RESONANT FREQUENCY BREATHING

**Purpose:** Resonant frequency breathing helps maximize heart rate variability (HRV), promoting emotional resilience and calming the nervous system. This technique involves finding your unique breath rate that feels most calming. Practice for 5-10 minutes a day.

1. **Relax Your Body:** Sit or lie down in a comfortable, quiet space.
2. **Begin Coherent Breathing:** Start by inhaling for 5-6 seconds and exhaling for 5-6 seconds.
3. **Find Your Resonant Frequency:** Experiment by slightly adjusting the inhale and exhale durations until you find the breath rate that feels the most calming and natural.
4. **Maintain Your Rhythm:** Once you've found your optimal breathing rate, continue breathing at this pace for the remainder of the session.
5. **Practice for 5-10 Minutes:** Focus on this breathing rhythm to fully engage your parasympathetic nervous system.

# EXTENDED EXHALATION BREATHING

**Purpose:** Extended exhalation breathing helps deepen relaxation by slowing the heart rate and activating the vagus nerve. This technique is particularly effective for reducing anxiety. Practice for 3-5 minutes a day or whenever you need quick relaxation.

1. **Find a Comfortable Position:** Sit or lie down, ensuring you're in a quiet and comfortable environment.
2. **Inhale for 4 sec Counts:** Breathe in through your nose for a slow count of 4 sec.
3. **Exhale for 8 sec Counts:** Breathe out through your mouth for a longer count of 8 sec.
4. **Focus on the Exhale:** Make sure your exhale is longer than your inhale to trigger deeper relaxation.
5. **Continue for 3-5 Minutes:** Repeat this breathing pattern, allowing your body to relax more deeply with each extended exhale.

# 4-7-8 BREATHING TECHNIQUE

**Purpose:** The 4-7-8 breathing technique is powerful for quickly reducing stress and promoting sleep. It also enhances vagal tone and supports emotional regulation. Practice this technique for 2-4 minutes, especially during moments of stress or before bed.

1. **Sit Comfortably:** Find a seated position with your back straight. Place the tip of your tongue behind your upper front teeth.
2. **Inhale for 4 Counts:** Breathe in quietly through your nose for a count of 4.
3. **Hold for 7 Counts:** Hold your breath for a count of 7.
4. **Exhale for 8 Counts:** Exhale entirely through your mouth for a count of 8, making a "whoosh" sound as you do.
5. **Repeat for 2-4 Minutes:** To start, perform this breathing cycle for 4 rounds, gradually increasing as you become more comfortable with the technique.

# WORKSHEET: VAGUS NERVE STIMULATION BREATHING TECHNIQUES

**Purpose:** This worksheet combines five powerful breathing exercises designed to stimulate the vagus nerve, calm the nervous system, and promote emotional regulation. Regular practice of these techniques enhances vagal tone, reduces stress, and supports overall well-being.

## STEP 1: CHOOSE YOUR BREATHING TECHNIQUE

Select one or more techniques to practice today:

- [ ] Diaphragmatic Breathing (Belly Breathing)
- [ ] Coherent Breathing
- [ ] 4-7-8 Breathing
- [ ] Resonant Frequency Breathing
- [ ] Extended Exhalation Breathing
- [ ] Other

# STEP 2: PRACTICE INSTRUCTIONS

## Diaphragmatic Breathing (Belly Breathing)

**Purpose:** Enhances vagal tone, reduces stress, and promotes relaxation.

| What did you notice about your breathing or emotional state? |
| --- |
|  |

## Coherent Breathing

**Purpose:** Balances the autonomic nervous system and increases heart rate variability (HRV).

| Did you feel more balanced or calm during this exercise? |
| --- |
|  |

## Resonant Frequency Breathing

**Purpose:** Maximizes HRV and supports emotional resilience.
Once you find your optimal breath rate, maintain it for 5-10 minutes.

| What was your optimal breathing rate, and how did it feel? |
| --- |
|  |

## Extended Exhalation Breathing

**Purpose:** Activates the vagus nerve by emphasizing longer exhalations to promote relaxation.

| Did you notice deeper relaxation or tension release with extended exhales? |
| --- |
|  |

## 4-7-8 Breathing Technique

**Purpose:** Quickly reduces stress, supports sleep, and enhances vagal tone.

| How did this technique affect your stress or energy levels? |
| --- |
|  |

# STEP 3: REFLECTION

**Which technique(s) felt most effective today? Why?**

**Did you notice any physical or emotional changes during or after the exercises?**

**How long did you practice in total?**

# PRACTICE LOG

| | |
|---|---|
| **Date &<br>Time of Day** | |
| **Techniques Practiced** | |
| **Duration of Practice** | |
| **Before Heart Rate Variability** | |
| **After Heart Rate Variability** | |
| **Effects Noticed** | |

## ADDITIONAL TIPS

- Practice daily to build your ability to activate the vagus nerve and calm the nervous system.
- Combine these techniques with other somatic therapies for enhanced emotional regulation.
- Pay attention to which technique works best for different situations, such as preparing for sleep or managing acute stress.

# GRADUAL COLD SHOWERS

**Purpose:** Cold showers are an easy way to begin incorporating cold exposure into your daily routine. They help build resilience, stimulate circulation, and activate the parasympathetic nervous system.

1. **Start with Warm Water:** Begin your shower with warm water to ease into the process and relax your muscles.
2. **Gradually Reduce the Temperature:** After a minute or two, slowly decrease the water temperature until it becomes cold. Start with water that feels cool but not unbearable.
3. **Time Your Exposure:** At first, stand under the cold water for 30 seconds to 1 minute. Gradually increase the duration as your body adjusts to the cold.
4. **Breathe Deeply:** Focus on slow, deep breaths with humming as you expose yourself to the cold water. This will help reduce any initial discomfort and promote relaxation.
5. **Increase Duration Gradually:** Over several days or weeks, try to increase the length of your cold showers by 15-30 seconds as your body becomes more acclimated.

# FACE IMMERSION IN COLD WATER

**Purpose:** Face immersion is a gentle way to practice cold exposure without the intensity of a full cold shower. It helps stimulate the vagus nerve and promotes a calming effect.

1. **Prepare the Basin:** Fill a basin or sink with cold water. You can add ice to make it colder, but ensure the water temperature is tolerable.
2. **Immerse Your Face:** Lower your face into the cold water and hold it there for 10-15 seconds. Breathe normally through your nose.
3. **Repeat the Process:** Lift your face out of the water, take a few deep breaths, and then repeat the immersion 2-3 times.
4. **Adjust as Needed:** As you get more comfortable, you can increase the duration of each immersion by 5 seconds but don't overdo it.

# ICE BATHS

**Purpose:** Purpose: Ice baths are a more advanced form of cold exposure that can build resilience, reduce inflammation, and improve recovery. Start slow and always proceed with caution.

1. **Prepare the Ice Bath:** Fill a bathtub with cold water, then gradually add ice until the water reaches a temperature of around 50-60°F (10-15°C).
2. **Start with Short Immersions:** Begin by submerging yourself in the ice bath for 1-2 minutes. Keep your head above the water to avoid cold shock.
3. **Listen to Your Body:** Pay attention to how your body feels. If you experience discomfort beyond initial coldness or start to shiver uncontrollably, exit the bath immediately.
4. **Have Someone Nearby:** Always ensure that someone is present when trying ice baths for the first time to monitor your safety.
5. **Gradually Increase Time:** You can gradually increase to longer immersions, but never push past what feels comfortable.

# SAFETY TIPS FOR COLD EXPOSURE

**Purpose:** Cold exposure can be powerful, but should always be approached with caution. Here are a few safety tips to keep in mind:

1. **Start Gradually:** Allow your body time to acclimatize to cold exposure.
2. **Listen to Your Body:** Never push past discomfort or shivering, as this can signify that your body is reaching its cold limit.
3. **Avoid Submerging Your Head:** Keep your head out of the water in ice baths to prevent shock.
4. **Consult a Healthcare Provider:** If you have any pre-existing health conditions, it is essential to consult a healthcare professional before starting a cold exposure routine.

# WORKSHEET: COLD EXPOSURE PRACTICES

Cold exposure is a powerful tool to build resilience, improve circulation, reduce inflammation, and promote emotional and physical well-being. This worksheet allows you to select your preferred cold exposure practice(s), track your sessions, and reflect on outcomes.

## STEP 1: CHOOSE YOUR TECHNIQUE(S)

Select one or more exercises to practice. Mark the one(s) you'll focus on today:

☐ **Gradual Cold Showers**

Start with warm water, then gradually reduce the temperature.

- Begin with 30 seconds to 1 minute under cold water, increasing duration over time.
- Focus on deep breathing to manage initial discomfort.

☐ **Face Immersion in Cold Water**

Fill a basin or sink with cold water (with or without ice).

- Immerse your face for 10-15 seconds, repeat 2-3 times.
- Gradually increase immersion time as comfortable.

☐ **Ice Baths**

Fill a tub with cold water and ice (50-60°F / 10-15°C).

- Submerge for 1-2 minutes, keeping your head above water.
- Gradually increase time as your body acclimates.

# STEP 2: SESSION DETAILS

Complete this section before and after each session.

| Date | Exercise Chosen | Duration | Mood Before | Mood After | Energy Levels | Notes on Experience |
|------|-----------------|----------|-------------|------------|---------------|---------------------|
|      |                 |          |             |            |               |                     |

# STEP 3: REFLECTION AND OUTCOMES

**Physical Effects:** Did you notice any improvements in circulation, muscle recovery, or energy levels?

**Emotional Effects:** How did the session impact your mood or stress levels?

**Challenges and Adjustments:** Were there any moments of discomfort, and how did you manage them?

**Mental Resilience:** Do you feel better equipped to handle challenges?

# STEP 3: REFLECTION AND OUTCOMES

Use this section to log your overall progress over time.

| Week | Techniques Used | Starting Duration | Current Duration | Notable Benefits | Areas to Improve |
|------|-----------------|-------------------|------------------|------------------|------------------|
|      |                 |                   |                  |                  |                  |
|      |                 |                   |                  |                  |                  |
|      |                 |                   |                  |                  |                  |
|      |                 |                   |                  |                  |                  |

## Safety Reminders:

Start gradually and build up your tolerance.
- Always listen to your body and stop if you feel overly uncomfortable or begin shivering uncontrollably.
- Consult a healthcare professional if you have pre-existing conditions.
- Ensure someone is nearby for safety during ice baths.

## Final Notes

Celebrate your progress! Consistency is key to unlocking the full benefits of cold exposure. Reflect on your journey, and let each session contribute to a healthier, more resilient you.

# HUMMING

1. **Find a Comfortable Position:** Sit or lie down in a relaxed, quiet space where you won't be disturbed.
2. **Close Your Eyes and Breathe:** Take a few deep breaths to center yourself.
3. **Start Humming a Tune:** Hum any simple tune that feels pleasant to you, such as a song or even a single tone. Focus on the vibrations you feel in your chest and throat as you hum.
4. **Focus on the Vibration:** To enhance the calming effect, pay attention to how the vibrations travel through your body, especially around your chest and throat.
5. **Repeat for 3-5 Minutes:** Hum for a few minutes, adjusting your pitch or tone if it feels right.

# CHANTING "OM"

**Purpose:** Chanting "OM" is a traditional vocal exercise that creates deep, resonant vibrations to stimulate the vagus nerve. This method promotes a deep sense of calm and connection to your body.

1. **Sit Comfortably:** Find a seated position with your spine straight, either on the floor or in a chair.
2. **Take a Deep Breath:** Inhale deeply through your nose.
3. **Chant "OM" Slowly:** As you exhale, chant "OM" slowly, allowing the sound to resonate for as long as possible. Focus on the vibrations it creates in your chest and throat.
4. **Repeat the Chant:** Take another deep breath and repeat the chant several times, paying attention to the soothing effect of the vibrations.
5. **Continue for 3-5 Minutes:** Chant for several minutes, letting yourself relax more deeply with each repetition.

# GARGLING

**Purpose:** Gargling is another simple method for stimulating the vagus nerve through gentle vibrations created in your throat. By engaging the parasympathetic nervous system, gargling helps to reduce stress, regulate emotions, and promote relaxation. It's easy to practice and can be done multiple times a day for consistent emotional support.

1. **Prepare a Sip of Water:** Take a small sip of water, ensuring it's at a comfortable temperature—not too hot or too cold.

2. **Tilt Your Head Back:** Tilt your head back so the water reaches the back of your throat.

3. **Start Gargling:** Begin to gargle, creating a steady, gentle vibration in your throat as you exhale through your mouth. Focus on keeping the sound rhythmic and smooth.

4. **Start with Short Sessions:** If you're new to gargling, begin with short sessions of 15-30 seconds to allow your throat muscles to adjust to the sensation.

5. **Gradually Increase Duration:** As you become more comfortable, gradually increase the duration by 10-15 seconds until you can gargle for up to a minute.

6. **Focus on the Vibrations:** Pay attention to the vibrations in your throat. They are key to engaging the vagus nerve and promoting a calming effect.

7. **Practice Multiple Times a Day:** You can incorporate gargling into your daily routine during your morning routine, after meals, or whenever you need a quick moment of relaxation.

Incorporating gargling into your daily routine helps stimulate the vagus nerve regularly, offering a simple yet effective way to support your emotional well-being.

# SINGING

> **Purpose:** Singing is another effective way to engage the vagus nerve. Whether in the shower or as part of your daily routine, singing helps regulate emotions and promote relaxation.

1. **Choose a Song You Enjoy:** Pick a song that feels uplifting or calming, whether it's a favorite tune or a simple melody.
2. **Find a Comfortable Space:** Sing where you feel comfortable, such as in the shower or in your car, where you can sing freely.
3. **Sing Slowly and Mindfully:** Focus on the act of singing, allowing yourself to fully experience the sound and vibration of your voice. Let the vibrations calm your body and mind.
4. **Immerse Yourself in the Moment:** Enjoy singing, relaxing, and letting go of any stress.
5. **Continue for a Few Minutes:** Sing for 3-5 minutes or longer if you have time.

# INCORPORATING VOCAL EXERCISES USE IN DAILY ROUTINE

> **Purpose:** Integrating vocal exercises can easily become part of your everyday routine, whether through singing, humming, or chanting.

1. **Sing in the Shower:** Let the acoustics and steam enhance your experience while enjoying the calming vibrations of your voice.
2. **Hum During Your Commute:** Turn your drive or commute into a moment of calm by humming to yourself, helping to reduce stress before or after work.
3. **Chant During Meditation:** Incorporate chanting "OM" into your meditation practice to deepen your relaxation and enhance your mind-body connection.
4. **Repeat Daily:** By adding these small moments to your day, you will notice a shift in positive emotional regulation and resilience over time.

# WORKSHEET: VOCAL EXERCISES FOR VAGUS NERVE STIMULATION

Vocal exercises like humming, chanting, gargling, and singing stimulate the vagus nerve through vibrations in the throat and chest, promoting relaxation, emotional balance, and stress reduction. Regular practice can help regulate the nervous system, enhance vagal tone, and improve overall well-being.

## STEP 1: CHOOSE YOUR VOCAL EXERCISE

Select one or more techniques to practice today:

- [ ] Humming
- [ ] Chanting "OM"
- [ ] Gargling
- [ ] Singing

## STEP 2: PRACTICE INSTRUCTIONS

### Humming

**Purpose:** Creates gentle vibrations to calm the nervous system and reduce stress.

**What did you notice about the vibrations or your emotional state?**

### Chanting "OM"

**Purpose:** Produces resonant vibrations to deeply relax the body and mind.

**What did you notice about the vibrations or your emotional state?**

# Gargling

**Purpose:** Stimulates the vagus nerve by creating throat vibrations and promoting relaxation.

**How did the vibrations from gargling impact your tension or stress levels?**

# Singing

**Purpose:** Combines vocal vibrations with emotional expression to regulate emotions and calm the nervous system.

**What emotions or sensations did you experience while singing?**

## STEP 3: INCORPORATE VOCAL EXERCISES INTO YOUR ROUTINE

**Daily Activities:** How will you add vocal exercises to your day? (Check all that apply)

- Sing in the shower to enhance relaxation with acoustics and steam.
- Hum during your commute to reduce stress before or after work.
- Chant "OM" during meditation to deepen relaxation and connection.
- Gargle as part of your morning or evening routine.

**Frequency:** How often will you practice these exercises?

**Goals:** What benefits are you hoping to achieve? (e.g., reduced stress, improved focus, better emotional regulation)

....................................................................................................

....................................................................................................

....................................................................................................

# STEP 4: REFLECTION AND NOTES

**Which vocal exercise(s) felt most effective today? Why?**

....................................................................................................

....................................................................................................

....................................................................................................

**Did you notice any physical or emotional changes during or after the exercises?**

....................................................................................................

....................................................................................................

....................................................................................................

**How long did you practice in total?**

....................................................................................................

....................................................................................................

....................................................................................................

# PRACTICE LOG

| Date | Exercises Practiced | Duration of Practice | Effects Noticed |
|------|---------------------|----------------------|-----------------|
|      |                     |                      |                 |
|      |                     |                      |                 |
|      |                     |                      |                 |
|      |                     |                      |                 |
|      |                     |                      |                 |

## ADDITIONAL TIPS

- Regularly practicing vocal exercises builds vagal tone and strengthens your ability to regulate emotions.
- Experiment with different methods to discover which works best for you.

Enjoy the process and let your voice be a tool for healing and connection!

# CHILD'S POSE (BALASANA)

> **Purpose:** Child's Pose is a restorative position that encourages deep relaxation and activates the vagus nerve by promoting slow, deep breathing.

1. **Start on Your Knees:** Kneel on the floor with your big toes touching and knees slightly apart.
2. **Sit Back on Your Heels:** Gently lower your hips to rest on your heels.
3. **Extend Your Arms Forward:** Reach your arms forward on the mat and lower your torso, bringing your forehead to rest on the mat.
4. **Focus on Your Breath:** Take slow, deep breaths, feeling your abdomen expand against your thighs. Let the gentle compression of your body calm your nervous system.
5. **Hold for 5-10 Breaths:** Stay in Child's Pose for several deep breaths, focusing on relaxation and releasing any tension in your body.

# CAT-COW POSE (MARJARYASANA-BITILASANA)

> **Purpose:** Cat-Cow Pose gently stretches the spine and promotes rhythmic movement paired with breath, helping to stimulate the vagus nerve.

1. **Get on Your Hands and Knees:** Start in a tabletop position with your wrists directly under your shoulders and knees under your hips.
2. **Inhale into Cow Pose:** As you inhale, arch your back, lift your chest, and gaze forward. Let your belly drop toward the mat.
3. **Exhale into Cat Pose:** As you exhale, round your spine, tuck your chin to your chest, and draw your belly toward your spine.
4. **Focus on the Rhythm:** Repeat this flow, moving with the rhythm of your breath, inhaling into Cow Pose, and exhaling into Cat Pose.
5. **Continue for 5-10 Rounds:** Perform this movement for several rounds, allowing your breath to guide each transition.

# BRIDGE POSE (SETU BANDHASANA)

**Purpose:** The Bridge Pose strengthens the back and legs while gently stimulating the vagus nerve through mindful breathing and opening the chest.

1. **Lie on Your Back:** Start by lying on your back with your knees bent and feet flat on the floor, hip-width apart.

2. **Press Through Your Feet:** Press your feet firmly into the ground and lift your hips toward the ceiling, keeping your shoulders grounded.

3. **Engage Your Core:** As you lift your hips, engage your core and glutes to support the pose. Keep your neck relaxed and chin slightly tucked.

4. **Breathe Deeply:** Take deep, rhythmic breaths, expanding your chest with each inhale.

5. **Hold for 5-7 Breaths:** Hold Bridge Pose for several breaths, then slowly lower your hips to the mat.

# WARRIOR I POSE (VIRABHADRASANA I)

**Purpose:** Warrior I is a standing pose that builds strength, balance, and focus while encouraging deep breathing and body awareness to engage the vagus nerve.

1. **Stand with Feet Wide Apart:** Stand tall with your feet wide apart, approximately three to four feet.

2. **Turn One Foot Outward:** Turn your right foot 90 degrees outward and angle your left foot slightly inward.

3. **Bend Your Front Knee:** Bend your right knee, ensuring it is aligned over your ankle. Keep your left leg straight.

4. **Extend Your Arms:** Raise both arms overhead, reaching toward the ceiling with your palms facing each other.

5. **Breathe Deeply:** Focus on taking deep, steady breaths as you hold the pose, feeling the strength in your body.

6. **Hold for 5-7 Breaths:** Hold Warrior I for several breaths, switch sides, and repeat on the other leg.

# WORKSHEET: YOGA PRACTICES FOR VAGUS NERVE STIMULATION (VNS)

**Purpose:** This worksheet is designed to help you reflect on your physical and emotional experiences before, during, and after practicing vagus nerve-stimulating yoga exercises. Use it to deepen your awareness of how these exercises affect your mood, body, and overall well-being.

## Exercise Log

### 1. Child's Pose (Balasana): Reflection Before Practice

| How do you feel physically? (e.g., tense, fatigued): | How do you feel emotionally? (e.g., anxious, calm, distracted) |
|---|---|
| | |

### During Practice

| What sensations do you notice in your body? (e.g., tension release). | How do you feel as you focus on your breathing? (e.g., calmer, more grounded): |
|---|---|
| | |

### Reflection After Practice

| How do you feel physically now? & How do you feel emotionally? | How does this pose compare to other relaxation methods you've tried? |
|---|---|
| | |

# 2. Cat-Cow Pose (Marjaryasana-Bitilasana)

## Reflection Before Practice

| How does your body feel as you prepare for this pose? (e.g., stiff, flexible): | How do you feel emotionally? |
|---|---|
| | |

## During Practice

| What sensations arise as you move through Cat and Cow poses? (e.g., spine stretch): | How does the rhythm of your breath affect your mood? |
|---|---|
| | |

## Reflection After Practice

| How do you feel physically after completing this pose? | How has your emotional state shifted? |
|---|---|
| | |

# 3. Bridge Pose (Setu Bandhasana)

## Reflection Before Practice

| How do your back and legs feel as you prepare for Bridge Pose? (e.g., tight, relaxed): | What emotions are you experiencing before starting? |
|---|---|
| | |

## During Practice

| How does your breathing feel as you hold the pose? (e.g., deep, shallow) | What physical sensations do you notice? (e.g., chest opening, leg engagement) |
|---|---|
| | |

## Reflection After Practice

| How do you feel physically? | How has your mood or energy shifted? |
|---|---|
| | |

# 4. Warrior I Pose (Virabhadrasana I)

## Reflection Before Practice

| How does your body feel aas you prepare for this pose? (e.g., balanced, unsteady) | What is your emotional state before beginning? (e.g., confident, anxious) |
|---|---|
| | |

## During Practice

| How does the strength and focus required for Warrior I affect your mood? | What physical sensations do you notice in your legs, arms, and core? |
|---|---|
| | |

## Reflection After Practice

| How does your body feel now? (e.g., stronger, lighter) | How has your mental state shifted? |
|---|---|
| | |

# REFLECTION QUESTIONS

**What surprised you most about your experience with these exercises?**

**Did you notice any common themes in your physical or emotional responses across the poses?**

**How will you incorporate these poses into your daily or weekly routine? (e.g., morning relaxation, stress relief after work).**

**Which pose felt most effective for vagus nerve stimulation today? Why?**

# DAILY PRACTICE SUMMARY

| | |
|---|---|
| **Date & Total Duration** | |
| **Poses Practiced** | |
| **Pre-exercise Heart Rate Variability** | |
| **Post-exercised Heart Rate Variability** | |
| **Emotional Observations** | |
| **Physical Observations** | |

## TIPS FOR CONSISTENCY AND GROWTH

- Track your practice over time to observe patterns in your physical and emotional responses.
- Focus on deep, intentional breathing during each pose to enhance vagus nerve stimulation.
- Combine these yoga practices with other VNS techniques for a more holistic approach to emotional balance and resilience.

Enjoy the calming and grounding benefits of these yoga poses!

# WORKSHEET: VAGUS NERVE STIMULATION (VNS) DEVICE USAGE LOG

**Purpose:** This worksheet helps you track and reflect on the effectiveness of your VNS device for managing stress, anxiety, mood, or other symptoms. Use it to monitor your progress and identify patterns over time.

## BEFORE THE SESSION

**Physical State:** How do you feel physically before using the VNS device? (e.g., tense, fatigued, restless)

**Emotional State:** How do you feel emotionally before using the VNS device? (e.g., anxious, calm, irritable):

## Reason for Using the Device Today

- [ ] Stress reduction
- [ ] Anxiety relief
- [ ] Improved focus
- [ ] Emotional regulation
- [ ] Other

## Symptom Intensity Rating (1–10)

| Stress | Anxiety | Mood (1 = very low, 10 = very positive) |
|--------|---------|------------------------------------------|
|        |         |                                          |

# DURING THE SESSION

**Experience During Use**

**How does the stimulation feel? (e.g., tingling, warmth, calming)**

**Did you notice any immediate physical changes? (e.g., slower heart rate, relaxed muscles)**

**Did you notice any immediate emotional changes? (e.g., reduced stress, better focus)**

## Comfort Level with the Device

- [ ] Very comfortable
- [ ] Neutral
- [ ] None
- [ ] Tingling sensation
- [ ] Slightly uncomfortable
- [ ] Uncomfortable
- [ ] Headache
- [ ] Other _____

## After the Session

**Physical State:** How do you feel physically after using the device? (e.g., relaxed, energized, no change)

**Emotional State:** How do you feel emotionally after using the device? (e.g., calm, uplifted, neutral)

### Symptom Intensity Rating (1–10)

| Stress | Anxiety | Mood (1 = very low, 10 = very positive) |
|---|---|---|
| | | |

**Overall Effectiveness:** How effective was the session in addressing your symptoms?

☐ Very effective          ☐ Moderately effective

☐ Slightly effective      ☐ Not effective

## WEEKLY REVIEW (OPTIONAL)

**How many sessions did you complete this week?**

**What patterns or changes did you notice in your symptoms over the week?**

**Which times of day or settings were most effective for using the device?**

**What adjustments will you make for next week?**

**Additional Notes:**
- Use this section to jot down any thoughts, observations, or questions to discuss with your healthcare provider or VNS specialist

**Tips for Effective Use**
- Use the device consistently at the same time each day to establish a routine.
- Pair VNS sessions with other calming activities, like deep breathing or meditation, for enhanced results.
- Monitor your progress regularly and share this worksheet with your healthcare provider to optimize your treatment plan.

Keep tracking your sessions to gain insight into how VNS improves your well-being over time!

# MID-BOOK REVIEW PAGE

## Your Experience Can Help Others!

*"You are never too insignificant to make a difference." – Gift Gugu Mona*

When I set out to write this book, my goal was always for it to be a workbook. I've heard so many people say that they've turned to self-help books but haven't felt like they've come away with a practical understanding of what they've read, and this is especially true for people who want to gather practical tools that will help them in their everyday lives.

There's certainly a place for theory, but with this book, I wanted to offer something more than that. I wanted my readers to be able to practice what they were learning in real time and make the entire process interactive from beginning to end. After all, somatic therapy is designed to be practiced; it isn't meant to stay stuck between the pages of a book.

The reason I've interrupted our journey here to tell you this is that I'd like to ask for your help. If you've been working through the exercises as you've been reading, you're probably already beginning to see how these techniques can help you, and you've probably reflected on a lot of things that have broadened your understanding of yourself.

This makes you the ideal person to help someone else discover this workbook and apply these techniques to their own life. Perhaps you know someone who might benefit from it, but even if you don't, you can still make a difference. You can help other people find it simply by leaving a short review.

***By leaving a review of this book on Amazon, you'll make it more likely that new readers will find the practical support they're looking for rather than stumbling on a theoretical book that doesn't give them the interactive experience they need.***

Reviews help connect books with the readers who need them the most, and your review could make a real difference, not least because you've been working through these exercises yourself and you know how effective they are.

Thank you so much for taking a moment to do this. I'd like to help as many people as I can, and with your support, I'll be able to reach more of them.

*Scan the QR code below to leave your review:*

# HRV EXERCISES FOR MENTAL HEALTH MANAGEMENT

Have you ever observed how a profound sense of calm sweeps over you at times of calm or how, in times of anxiety, your heart seems to race? That is your heart rate reacting to your physical and mental conditions. What if you could change this relationship to enhance your mental well-being? Here comes heart rate variability (HRV), a powerful yet sometimes disregarded indicator of your body's stress tolerance and emotional balance.

HRV is the small changes in the intervals between your heartbeats. A higher HRV typically indicates good physical and mental health because it shows how well your body can adjust to stressors. Conversely, a lower HRV can indicate that your system has trouble properly regulating emotions or recovering from stress. The good news? Although HRV cannot be changed, it can be improved through deliberate actions.

Think of your HRV like a muscle. HRV exercises support the development of emotional and mental resilience, much like physical exercise does for your body. For example, mindfulness and meditation balance your parasympathetic (rest-and-digest) and sympathetic (fight-or-flight) systems, while deep, rhythmic breathing can help control your heart rate. These techniques can improve your capacity to manage stress and sustain a consistent sense of well-being over time.

Visualize being stuck in a traffic jam, feeling your frustration build. Rather than allowing the stress to take over, you concentrate on slowing your breathing, inhaling for four counts and exhaling for six. You might be unable to move your car, but you can change your emotional condition. The value of HRV exercises is in their ability to provide you with control during situations that could otherwise feel overpowering.

This activity will walk you through techniques to raise your HRV and, consequently, your mental well-being. With regular practice, you'll feel more emotionally stable and grounded and be more capable of handling challenges in life.

# RESONANCE FREQUENCY BREATHING

**Purpose:** Resonance Frequency Breathing is a powerful technique that synchronizes your heart rate with your breath to optimize heart rate variability (HRV). You create a harmonious rhythm that activates the parasympathetic nervous system by breathing at a specific pace, typically five to seven breaths per minute. This practice reduces stress and anxiety, improves emotional regulation, promotes relaxation, and strengthens resilience to life's challenges. Physically, it enhances cardiovascular health and helps regulate the body's response to stress, making it an ideal exercise for mental and physical well-being.

1. **Find a Comfortable Position:** Sit or lie down comfortably with your back supported. Close your eyes and begin with a few deep, centering breaths to prepare yourself for the exercise.

2. **Set Up Your HRV Device:** Attach your HRV sensor and start your monitoring device. Make sure it is tracking your heart rate variability so you can monitor changes throughout the exercise.

3. **Breathe at Your Resonant Frequency:** Inhale deeply through your nose for a count of five. Hold your breath briefly, then exhale slowly through your mouth for a count of five. The goal is to achieve a breathing rate of five to seven breaths per minute. Continue this pattern, synchronizing your breath with your heart rate to optimize your HRV.

4. **Monitor HRV Feedback:** Watch the feedback on your device and note how your HRV responds to this specific breathing rhythm. Aim for a steady, coherent heart rate pattern that reflects improved HRV.

5. **Practice for 10-20 Minutes:** Continue resonance frequency breathing for 10 to 20 minutes. As your HRV improves, you should feel a deep sense of calm and emotional balance.

# DIAPHRAGMATIC BREATHING

**Purpose:** Diaphragmatic breathing, or deep belly breathing, is a simple yet highly effective technique that stimulates the parasympathetic nervous system, promoting a state of calm and relaxation. By breathing deeply into the diaphragm, you engage your body's natural "rest and digest" response, which helps reduce stress, lower heart rate, and enhance overall emotional stability. This technique eases anxiety and tension, improves lung function, lowers blood pressure, and supports a balanced nervous system. It is a powerful tool for both mental clarity and physical health.

1. **Sit or Lie Down Comfortably:** Find a quiet space where you can sit with your back straight or lie down comfortably with your arms resting at your sides. Close your eyes and take a few slow breaths to center yourself.

2. **Start the HRV Monitoring Device:** Begin the HRV monitoring on your device or app to track your progress. Ensure the sensor is attached and calibrated correctly to monitor your heart rate variability.

3. **Breathe into Your Diaphragm:** Place one hand on your chest and the other on your abdomen. Inhale deeply through your nose, allowing your diaphragm to expand fully while keeping your chest still. Your abdomen should rise with each breath. Hold your breath briefly, then slowly exhale through your mouth, feeling your abdomen fall. Focus on making each exhalation longer than your inhalation to engage the parasympathetic nervous system.

4. **Focus on HRV Feedback:** As you breathe deeply, pay attention to the real-time HRV feedback from your device. Notice how your HRV improves as you relax into the breathing rhythm.

5. **Practice for 10-20 Minutes:** Continue diaphragmatic breathing for 10 to 20 minutes, allowing your body to relax fully. Your HRV should stabilize and increase, signaling a shift into a more relaxed state.

# WORKSHEET: HRV BIOFEEDBACK BREATHING EXERCISES

> **Purpose:** Diaphragmatic breathing, or deep belly breathing, is a simple yet highly effective technique that stimulates the parasympathetic nervous system, promoting a state of calm and relaxation. By breathing deeply into the diaphragm, you engage your body's natural "rest and digest" response, which helps reduce stress, lower heart rate, and enhance overall emotional stability. This technique eases anxiety and tension, improves lung function, lowers blood pressure, and supports a balanced nervous system. It is a powerful tool for both mental clarity and physical health.

## Step 1: Prepare for Your Session

**Find a Comfortable Position:**

- Sit or lie down in a quiet space with your back supported.
- Close your eyes and take a few deep, centering breaths to prepare.

**Set Up Your HRV Monitoring Device:**

- Attach your HRV sensor securely.
- Ensure your device or app is calibrated and tracking your heart rate variability.

> **Set Your Intentions: Why are you practicing HRV breathing today? (e.g., reduce stress, enhance focus, improve emotional regulation):**

## Step 2: Practice the Breathing Exercises

**Resonance Frequency Breathing**

Purpose: Synchronize your heart rate with your breath to achieve optimal HRV.

**Breathing Pattern:**

- Inhale deeply through your nose for a count of 5.
- Hold your breath briefly.
- Exhale slowly through your mouth for a count of 5.
- Continue breathing at this rhythm (5-7 breaths per minute).

**What sensations do you notice as you synchronize your breath with your HRV?**

**How does your HRV feedback change throughout the exercise? (e.g., steady heart rate, higher coherence):**

## Diaphragmatic Breathing

**Purpose:** Activates the parasympathetic nervous system to promote calm and relaxation.

**Breathing Pattern:**

- Place one hand on your chest and the other on your abdomen.
- Inhale deeply through your nose allowing your abdomen to rise while keeping your chest still.
- Hold your breath briefly then exhale slowly through your mouth feeling your abdomen fall.
- I'd like you to focus on making each exhalation longer than your inhalation.

**How does your abdominal movement change as you focus on diaphragmatic breathing?**

**What changes do you notice in your HRV feedback during this exercise? (e.g., more stability, increased HRV):**

# Step 3: Monitor and Reflect on HRV Feedback

**Real-Time Feedback: What trends did you observe in your HRV during the session? (e.g., consistent improvement, sudden shifts).**

**Physical Sensations: Did you feel more relaxed, energized, or balanced after the exercises?**

**Emotional Observations: How did your emotional state change during or after the session? (e.g., reduced anxiety, enhanced focus, greater calm).**

# Step 4: Evaluate Your Progress

**Overall Effectiveness of Today's Practice:**

☐ Very Effective

☐ Moderately Effective

☐ Slightly Effective

☐ Not Effective

# SYMPTOM INTENSITY RATING (1–10):

## Before Session

| Stress | Anxiety | Mood (1 = very low, 10 = very positive) | Pre-exercise Heart Rate Variability |
|--------|---------|-----------------------------------------|-------------------------------------|
|        |         |                                         |                                     |

## After Session

| Stress | Anxiety | Mood (1 = very low, 10 = very positive) | Pre-exercise Heart Rate Variability |
|---|---|---|---|
|  |  |  |  |

## STEP 5: PLAN FOR NEXT TIME

**Adjustments to Your Practice: What would you change about your session for next time? (e.g., longer duration, different breathing rhythm).**

**Frequency of Practice: How often will you incorporate these exercises into your routine? (e.g., daily, 3 times per week).**

**Goals for Your Next Session: What do you hope to achieve? (e.g., higher HRV, reduced stress, better focus).**

# DAILY PRACTICE SUMMARY

| | |
|---|---|
| **Date** | |
| **Exercises Practiced** | |
| **Total Duration** | |
| **HRV Trends Observed** | |
| **Physical Changes** | |
| **Emotional Changes** | |

## TIPS FOR CONSISTENCY AND GROWTH

- Use consistent timing for your sessions to track progress effectively.
- Combine these exercises with other mindfulness techniques, such as meditation, for enhanced benefits.
- Could you share your HRV data with a healthcare provider to tailor your practice for specific goals?
- By regularly practicing HRV biofeedback breathing, you'll strengthen your ability to regulate emotions, reduce stress, and improve overall resilience!

# GUIDED IMAGERY

**Purpose:** Guided imagery is a therapeutic technique that combines deep breathing with vivid mental visualization to promote emotional healing and optimize heart rate variability (HRV). By immersing yourself in a peaceful, imagined setting, such as a serene beach or a tranquil forest, you engage your senses and shift your mind from stress to relaxation. This practice enhances emotional resilience, reduces anxiety, and fosters physical healing by improving HRV. Guided imagery helps calm the nervous system, making it a valuable tool for emotional well-being and physical balance.

1. **Prepare Your Space:** Sit or lie down in a quiet, comfortable area. Close your eyes and take a few deep breaths, allowing your body to relax.

2. **Begin HRV Monitoring:** Start your HRV device to track your heart rate variability during the guided imagery exercise.

3. **Visualize a Calming Scene:** As you breathe deeply, imagine yourself in a peaceful setting—a beach, a forest, or any place that brings you a sense of calm. Engage all your senses. Feel the warmth of the sun, hear the gentle waves, or smell the fresh air.

4. **Sync Your Breathing with the Imagery:** Continue breathing deeply and slowly as you immerse yourself in the calming imagery. Imagine the air you breathe in is filled with peace, and with each exhalation, release tension and stress.

5. **Monitor HRV:** Watch your HRV feedback as you deepen your visualization and breathing. Notice how your heart rate variability improves as your mind and body relax into the imagery.

6. **Practice for 10-20 Minutes:** Continue the guided imagery exercise for 10 to 20 minutes, letting yourself fully immerse in the scene and enjoying the calming effects on your HRV.

# WORKSHEET: HRV BIOFEEDBACK WITH GUIDED IMAGERY

**Purpose:** This worksheet helps you combine guided imagery with HRV biofeedback to enhance relaxation, improve heart rate variability (HRV), and promote emotional and physical well-being. By visualizing peaceful settings while monitoring your HRV, you can track your progress and deepen your relaxation.

## STEP 1: PREPARE YOUR SPACE

Where are you practicing this session? (e.g., bedroom, quiet corner, outdoor space)

What steps did you take to prepare? (e.g., dimmed lights, turned off distractions)

### Starting Emotional State

How do you feel emotionally before starting? (e.g., anxious, calm, distracted)

### Starting Physical State

How does your body feel before starting? (e.g., tense, relaxed, restless)

## STEP 2: GUIDED IMAGERY EXERCISE

**Describe Your Visualization**

What setting did you choose to imagine? (e.g., beach, forest, meadow)

What sensory details did you incorporate? (e.g., sound of waves, smell of flowers, warmth of the sun)

## Breathing Pattern

Describe your breathing rhythm during the exercise: (e.g., slow and deep, synchronized with imagery)

**HRV Monitoring Feedback:** How did your HRV change as you visualized the calming scene? (e.g., more stable, increased coherence)

# STEP 3: REFLECTION DURING PRACTICE

| Emotional Shifts: What emotions arose during the exercise? (e.g., peace, joy, nostalgia) |
| --- |
| |

| Physical Sensations: How did your body respond to the visualization? (e.g., tension release, slower heart rate) |
| --- |
| |

| HRV Trends Observed: Did your HRV improve during the exercise? (e.g., steady improvement, fluctuations) |
| --- |
| |

# Step 4: Post-Practice Reflection

**Ending Emotional State: How do you feel emotionally after completing the session? (e.g., calmer, more focused)**

**Ending Physical State: How does your body feel now? (e.g., lighter, less tense, more relaxed)**

## Final HRV Reading

**What was your HRV at the end of the session?**

**How does this compare to your baseline? (e.g., higher, steadier)**

## Overall Evaluation

Effectiveness of Guided Imagery for HRV Improvement

☐ Very Effective          ☐ Moderately Effective

☐ Slightly Effective      ☐ Not Effective

**What part of the exercise felt most impactful?**

**What adjustments would you make for your next session?**

# DAILY PRACTICE SUMMARY

| Session Duration | Visualization Setting Used | HRV Changes Observed | Emotional/Physical Changes Noted |
|---|---|---|---|
|  |  |  |  |
|  |  |  |  |
|  |  |  |  |
|  |  |  |  |
|  |  |  |  |

## SESSION DETAILS

| Date | Time of Session | HRV Device Used | Baseline HRV Reading |
|---|---|---|---|
|  |  |  |  |

## TIPS FOR FUTURE PRACTICE

- Use vivid sensory details in your visualization to fully engage your mind and body.
- Pair the exercise with soothing background music or nature sounds for enhanced immersion.
- Practice consistently, tracking your HRV over time to identify patterns in your emotional and physical responses.

# PROGRESSIVE MUSCLE RELAXATION (PMR)

**Purpose:** Progressive Muscle Relaxation (PMR) is an effective technique that involves tensing and relaxing each muscle group to reduce physical tension and stress. By consciously working through the body—from your toes to your head—you release muscle tightness and activate the parasympathetic nervous system, which promotes relaxation and improves heart rate variability (HRV). PMR is highly beneficial for managing anxiety, relieving stress, and promoting better sleep. Mentally, it helps increase awareness of where your body holds tension, empowering you to release it for greater physical and emotional balance.

1. **Find a Relaxed Position:** Sit or lie down in a quiet space. Make sure you are comfortable, with your arms at your sides, and your eyes closed.

2. **Start HRV Monitoring:** Turn on your HRV biofeedback device and ensure the sensor is attached correctly. This will allow you to track changes in your HRV as you release tension from your body.

3. **Tense and Relax Each Muscle Group:** Start with your toes. Tense the muscles for 5-10 seconds, then release, exhaling deeply as you relax the muscles completely. Work your way up through each muscle group—feet, calves, thighs, abdomen, chest, arms, shoulders, neck, and face—tensing and relaxing each group in turn.

4. **Pay Attention to HRV Feedback:** As you move through each muscle group, observe how tensing and relaxing affect your HRV. Notice the improvement in your heart rate variability as you release tension.

5. **Practice for 10-20 Minutes:** Continue the exercise for 10 to 20 minutes, allowing your HRV to stabilize and increase as your body fully relaxes.

# WORKSHEET: HRV BIOFEEDBACK WITH PROGRESSIVE MUSCLE RELAXATION (PMR)

This worksheet guides you through Progressive Muscle Relaxation (PMR) with an emphasis on heart rate variability (HRV). By tensing and relaxing each muscle group while monitoring your HRV, you can track physical and emotional improvements as tension is released, and relaxation deepens.

## STEP 1: PREPARE FOR THE SESSION

**Where are you practicing? (e.g., bed, yoga mat, recliner)**

**How did you create a relaxing space? (e.g., dim lighting, quiet, soothing music)**

### Initial Emotional State

**How do you feel emotionally before starting? (e.g., anxious, stressed, calm)**

### Initial Physical State

**How does your body feel before starting? (e.g., tense shoulders, tight jaw, relaxed)**

## STEP 2: PERFORM PROGRESSIVE MUSCLE RELAXATION

### Muscle Groups: Toes and Feet

| Tension Level Before | Relaxation Sensations After | HRV Feedback Observations |
|---|---|---|
|  |  |  |

### Calves and Thighs

| Tension Level Before | Relaxation Sensations After | HRV Feedback Observations |
|---|---|---|
|  |  |  |

## Abdomen and Chest

| Tension Level Before | Relaxation Sensations After | HRV Feedback Observations |
|---|---|---|
|  |  |  |

## Arms and Shoulders

| Tension Level Before | Relaxation Sensations After | HRV Feedback Observations |
|---|---|---|
|  |  |  |

## Neck and Face

| Tension Level Before | Relaxation Sensations After | HRV Feedback Observations |
|---|---|---|
|  |  |  |

# STEP 3: MONITOR HRV AND REFLECT

### Real-Time HRV Changes

Did your HRV improve as you worked through the muscle groups? (e.g., smoother coherence, higher variability)

### Emotional Changes

How did your mood change during the exercise? (e.g., calmer, less overwhelmed)

### Physical Awareness

Did you notice a physical shift after releasing tension?

Were you surprised by the level of tension in any particular area?

# STEP 4: POST-PRACTICE REFLECTION

**Ending Emotional State: How do you feel emotionally now? (e.g., peaceful, neutral, lighter)**

**Ending Physical State: How does your body feel now? (e.g., less tense, relaxed, comfortable)**

## Final HRV Reading

**What was your HRV at the end of the session?**

**How does it compare to your baseline? (e.g., improved, steady)**

## Overall Evaluation

Effectiveness of PMR for HRV Improvement

- [ ] Very Effective
- [ ] Moderately Effective
- [ ] Slightly Effective
- [ ] Not Effective

**What part of the exercise felt most beneficial?**

**What adjustments will you make for your next session?**

## SESSION DETAILS

| Date | Time of Session | HRV Device Used | Baseline HRV Reading |
|------|-----------------|-----------------|----------------------|
|      |                 |                 |                      |

## DAILY PRACTICE SUMMARY

| | |
|---|---|
| **Session Duration** | |
| **HRV Observations** | |
| **Physical/Emotional Changes Noted** | |

## TIPS FOR FUTURE PRACTICE

- Practice PMR consistently to track long-term improvements in HRV and relaxation.
- Pay attention to areas of chronic tension and observe patterns in HRV responses.
- Combine PMR with other relaxation techniques, such as guided imagery or diaphragmatic breathing, for enhanced benefits.
- Enjoy the calming effects of Progressive Muscle Relaxation while monitoring your HRV for measurable results!

# NEUROSOMATIC THERAPY: THE ULTIMATE 30-MINUTE HEALING FORMULA

What if you could spend thirty minutes rewiring your body and mind to relieve tension, release stress, and restore balance? That is the strength of NeuroSomatic Therapy, a revolutionary technique that fosters healing by establishing a connection between the body and brain. This technique helps you overcome stress cycles and access your natural healing potential by treating the neurological system and physical sensations.

The body often shows signs of stress and trauma, such as tense shoulders, clinched jaws, or a racing heart. Your nervous system uses these physical symptoms to let you know it's out of sync. NeuroSomatic Therapy creates a complete reset by combining techniques that soothe the body and quiet the mind. It's like allowing your body and brain to "speak" to one another, creating a foundation of balance and safety.

Imagine this: Your body feels heavy and stiff, and your mind replays unpleasant scenes from your difficult day. Rather than ignoring it or pushing through it, you stop and begin this 30-minute healing practice. You observe that your body relaxes, and your thoughts become clearer when you practice mindful awareness, gentle movements, and focused breathing. Ultimately, you feel lighter, more in control, and prepared to go on.

This exercise incorporates various Neuro-somatic techniques, including guided meditations, rhythmic breathing, and targeted physical movements that help release pent-up tension. It's not just about relaxing; it's about making a long-lasting difference in how your body and brain react to stress. These techniques can help you become more emotionally resilient, focus better, and regain inner calm over time.

This 30-minute healing formula is made to meet you where you are, whether you're recovering from a difficult event, dealing with residual stress, or just wanting to relax. It's a strong, effective technique for resetting your nervous system and reestablishing your connection to your entire self.

# NEUROSOMATIC EXERCISES FOR ANXIETY, STRESS, AND TRAUMA

**Purpose:** This subchapter focuses on practical, step-by-step NeuroSomatic exercises that can be completed in less than 30 minutes a day to help manage anxiety, stress, trauma, and physical health challenges. Each exercise combines proven techniques like deep breathing, grounding, vagus nerve stimulation, and HRV biofeedback to create a quick and effective daily routine. Designed for ease of use, these exercises empower you to take control of your emotional and physical well-being, providing immediate relief while building long-term resilience.

## Grounding with Diaphragmatic Breathing

**Purpose:** This exercise provides immediate relief from anxiety and stress by grounding you in the present moment and calming your nervous system through deep breathing and physical connection.

1. **Get Comfortable:** Sit or stand in a comfortable position where you can focus.
2. 5-4-3-2-1 Grounding Technique: Identify:

- Five things you can see.
- Four things you can touch.
- Three things you can hear.
- Two things you can smell.
- One thing you can taste.

3. **Incorporate Deep Breathing:** Practice slow belly breathing throughout, focusing on expanding your abdomen as you inhale and relaxing it as you exhale.
4. **Add Vagus Nerve Stimulation:** On each exhale, hum gently to activate your vagus nerve and deepen relaxation.
5. **Use Biofeedback:** Monitor your HRV with a biofeedback device, adjusting your breathing to maintain a steady, calm rhythm.
6. **Repeat as Needed:** Perform this exercise until you feel calmer and more relaxed.

# WORKSHEET: NEUROSOMATIC EXERCISES FOR ANXIETY, STRESS AND TRAUMA

This worksheet guides you through a daily NeuroSomatic exercise designed to address anxiety, stress, trauma, and physical health challenges. By combining grounding techniques, diaphragmatic breathing, vagus nerve stimulation, and HRV biofeedback, you can create an effective and time-efficient practice to improve emotional and physical well-being.

## STEP 1: GROUNDING WITH THE 5-4-3-2-1 TECHNIQUE

**Describe Your Environment: Where are you practicing? (e.g., living room, park, bedroom).**

## STEP 2: INCORPORATE DIAPHRAGMATIC BREATHING

### Breathing Observations

| How does your abdomen move with each breath? (e.g., expanding, shallow, rhythmic). | What sensations do you notice as you focus on your breath? (e.g., relaxation, warmth, calmness). |
|---|---|
| | |

### HRV Feedback (if using a device)

| How does your HRV change during diaphragmatic breathing? (e.g., increased coherence, steadier rhythm). |
|---|
| |

# STEP 3: ADD VAGUS NERVE STIMULATION

## Humming Observations

| Describe the sensations in your chest and throat as you hum on each exhale. (e.g., vibrations, soothing effect). | How does humming affect your sense of relaxation or calm? |
|---|---|
| | |

## HRV Feedback (if applicable)

| Did humming improve your HRV measurements? (e.g., higher variability, steady patterns). |
|---|
| |

# STEP 4: REPEAT AND REFLECT

| Time Spent on the Exercise | Total duration of practice |
|---|---|
| | |

| Physical Observations: How does your body feel after completing the exercise? (e.g., less tense, more grounded) | Emotional Observations: How does your emotional state compare to when you started? (e.g., calmer, clearer, more stable). |
|---|---|
| | |

| Final HRV Reading (if using a device) | Improvement from initial reading |
|---|---|
| | |

## Overall Reflections and Notes

| What part of the exercise was most effective for you? Why? | Did you encounter any challenges during the exercise? How will you address them next time? |
|---|---|
| | |

| How will you incorporate this exercise into your daily routine? (e.g., morning practice, midday stress relief, evening relaxation). |
|---|
| |

# GOALS FOR NEXT WEEK

| What adjustments or additions will you make to your practice? |
|---|
| |

| Tips for Success |
|---|
| 1. .................................................................................................................. <br> 2. .................................................................................................................. <br> 3. .................................................................................................................. |

**Consistency is key:**

- Practice this exercise daily to build resilience and improve your HRV over time.
- Use a journal or this worksheet regularly to track your progress and identify patterns.
- Combine this exercise with other NeuroSomatic techniques for a more comprehensive approach to emotional and physical well-being.
- By integrating this quick and effective exercise into your routine, you can create a powerful tool for managing anxiety, stress, trauma, and physical health challenges.

# PROGRESSIVE MUSCLE RELAXATION (PMR) WITH RESONANT FREQUENCY BREATHING

**Purpose:** This exercise helps release physical tension and promotes emotional calm by combining muscle relaxation with rhythmic breathing, effectively managing anxiety and reducing stress.

1. **Find a Quiet Space:** Sit or lie down in a quiet, comfortable spot.
2. **Tense and Relax Muscles:** Start with your feet, tensing each muscle group for a few seconds, then relax. Move upward through your body, ending with your face and head.
3. **Practice Resonant Breathing:** Inhale for five counts, hold briefly, and exhale for five counts.
4. **Monitor Your HRV:** Use a biofeedback device to track the reduction in anxiety levels and fine-tune your breathing.
5. **Repeat as Needed:** Perform this exercise until you feel calmer and more relaxed.

## WORKSHEET: NEUROSOMATIC THERAPY – PMR WITH RESONANT

**Frequency Breathing:** This worksheet helps you combine Progressive Muscle Relaxation (PMR) with Resonant Frequency Breathing to release physical tension, promote emotional calm, and manage anxiety. The integration of HRV biofeedback allows you to track and optimize your relaxation and stress reduction.

| Date | Time of Session | HRV Device Used | Baseline HRV Reading |
|------|-----------------|-----------------|----------------------|
|      |                 |                 |                      |

159

## STEP 1: PREPARE YOUR SPACE

### Environment Description

Where are you practicing?
(e.g., bedroom, quiet office, yoga mat).

How did you prepare the space? (e.g., dimmed lights, added soothing music).

Initial Emotional State: How do you feel emotionally before starting? (e.g., anxious, overwhelmed).

Initial Physical State: How does your body feel before starting? (e.g., tense, fatigued).

# STEP 2: PROGRESSIVE MUSCLE RELAXATION (PMR)

## Muscle Groups

### Feet and Ankles

Tense: How did it feel to tense this area? (e.g., tight, neutral)

Relax: How did relaxation feel? (e.g., release of tension, lighter)

### Legs (Calves and Thighs)

Tense: How did it feel to tense this area? (e.g., tight, neutral)

Relax: How did relaxation feel? (e.g., release of tension, lighter)

### Abdomen and Chest

Tense: How did it feel to tense this area? (e.g., tight, neutral)

Relax: How did relaxation feel? (e.g., release of tension, lighter)

## Arms and Shoulders

| Tense: How did it feel to tense this area? (e.g., tight, neutral) | Relax: How did relaxation feel? (e.g., release of tension, lighter) |
|---|---|
| | |

## Neck and Face

| Tense: How did it feel to tense this area? (e.g., tight, neutral) | Relax: How did relaxation feel? (e.g., release of tension, lighter) |
|---|---|
| | |

**Overall Sensations After PMR: Did you notice a difference in tension levels after working through your muscles?**

.........................................................................................................................................................

.........................................................................................................................................................

.........................................................................................................................................................

.........................................................................................................................................................

# STEP 3: RESONANT FREQUENCY BREATHING

**Breathing Pattern:**

Inhale for 5 counts, hold briefly, exhale for 5 counts.

## Observations During Practice

| How did the rhythm of your breath feel? (e.g., steady, difficult, calming) | What physical sensations did you notice during breathing? (e.g., chest expansion, warmth) |
|---|---|
| | |

........................................................................................

........................................................................................

........................................................................................

## STEP 4: REFLECTION AND OUTCOMES

**Emotional Changes: How did your emotional state shift after completing the exercise? (e.g., calmer, more grounded)**

**Physical Changes: How does your body feel now compared to when you started? (e.g., less tense, lighter)**

**Final HRV Reading**

**Improvement from baseline**

### Overall Effectiveness

How effective was this exercise in reducing anxiety or promoting relaxation?

- ☐ Very Effective
- ☐ Moderately Effective
- ☐ Slightly Effective
- ☐ Not Effective

# Trends Over Time

**Which muscle groups consistently hold the most tension?**

**Does PMR combined with Resonant Breathing result in noticeable HRV improvements?**

**Favorite Components: Which aspect of this exercise (PMR or Resonant Breathing) feels most impactful for you?**

**Adjustments for Next Practice: What will you change or focus on during your next session? (e.g., longer sessions).**

## Tips for Success

- **Consistency:** Practice this exercise daily or as needed to build long-term resilience.
- **Mind-Body Awareness:** Pay attention to where your body holds tension and how HRV changes reflect your progress.
- **Customization:** Adjust the breathing pattern or duration to suit your comfort level and needs.

- Enjoy the calming and restorative effects of PMR combined with Resonant Breathing!

# BODY SCAN WITH VAGUS NERVE STIMULATION

**Purpose:** This exercise fosters deep relaxation and reduces stress by combining body awareness with vagus nerve stimulation, helping to alleviate anxious sensations and promote emotional balance.

1. **Lie or Sit Comfortably:** Choose a position that allows you to focus on your body.
2. **Begin a Body Scan:** Slowly shift your attention to each part of your body, starting from your head and moving to your toes.
3. **Deep Breathing:** Maintain deep belly breathing throughout the exercise.
4. **Add Vocalization:** Use gentle humming or chanting to stimulate the vagus nerve and enhance relaxation.
5. **Track Your HRV:** Monitor your HRV to observe stress reduction and track progress over time.
6. **Repeat as Needed:** Perform this exercise until you feel calmer and more relaxed.

# ALTERNATE NOSTRIL BREATHING WITH SENSORY GROUNDING

**Purpose:** This exercise helps calm the mind and reduce anxiety by combining breath regulation with sensory grounding, providing a comprehensive approach to managing stress and enhancing focus.

1. **Sit Comfortably:** Hold a textured object in one hand for sensory grounding.
2. **Practice Alternate Nostril Breathing:**
- Close one nostril with your finger and inhale through the open nostril.
- Switch nostrils and exhale through the opposite nostril.
3. **Combine Breathing with Touch:** Focus on the object's texture as you breathe to further distract from anxious thoughts.
4. **Monitor Your HRV:** Use a biofeedback device to track the calming effects of the exercise.
5. **Repeat Until Calm:** Continue until you feel grounded and relaxed.

# WORKSHEET: NEUROSOMATIC THERAPY – BODY SCAN WITH VNS & SENSORY BREATHING

> **Purpose:** This worksheet combines two powerful NeuroSomatic exercises: a body scan with vagus nerve stimulation and alternate nostril breathing with sensory grounding. These exercises help reduce stress, manage anxiety, and promote emotional balance by integrating mindfulness, breathing, and HRV biofeedback.

| Date | Time of Session | HRV Device Used | Baseline HRV Reading |
|------|-----------------|-----------------|----------------------|
|      |                 |                 |                      |

**Position: Are you lying or sitting? (e.g., lying on a mat, sitting in a chair)**

## Initial State

| How do you feel physically before starting? (e.g., tense, restless) | How do you feel emotionally before starting? (e.g., anxious, neutral) |
|---|---|
|   |   |

## Body Scan Observations

What sensations did you notice in each area of your body?

| Head and Face |  |
|---|---|
| **Shoulders and Arms** |  |
| **Chest and Abdomen** |  |
| **Legs and Feet** |  |

# Vagus Nerve Stimulation

Describe the sensations during humming or chanting. (e.g., vibrations, calming effect)

Did vocalization enhance your relaxation? (e.g., yes, slightly, not sure)

HRV Feedback: How did your HRV change during this exercise? (e.g., steady increase, fluctuations).

# EXERCISE 2: ALTERNATE NOSTRIL BREATHING WITH SENSORY GROUNDING

Where are you sitting? (e.g., desk, meditation cushion).

What object are you using for sensory grounding? (e.g., stress ball, textured rock).

## Breathing and Sensory Integration

Describe the texture of the object. (e.g., smooth, rough, soft).

How did focusing on the texture help distract from anxious thoughts?

## Alternate Nostril Breathing

How did this breathing technique feel? (e.g., calming, challenging, neutral).

Did you notice any physical or emotional changes during the breathing?

**HRV Feedback: What trends did you observe in your HRV during this exercise? (e.g., increased coherence, steadiness).**

## Outcome

| Duration of Practice | Emotional State After | Physical State After |
| --- | --- | --- |
| | | |

## Reflection and Long-Term Tracking

**Which exercise felt most effective for you today? Why?**

## HRV Improvement

| Baseline HRV | Final HRV After Exercises | Change in HRV |
| --- | --- | --- |
| | | |

**Trends Observed Over Time: Which exercise helps most with anxiety reduction?**

# WEEKLY SUMMARY (OPTIONAL)

| Date | Exercise Practiced | Duration | Baseline HRV | Post Session HRV | Emotional/Physical Observation |
|------|--------------------|----------|--------------|------------------|-------------------------------|
|      |                    |          |              |                  |                               |
|      |                    |          |              |                  |                               |
|      |                    |          |              |                  |                               |

**Adjustments for Future Sessions: What will you modify or try differently next time? (e.g., longer sessions, focus on specific techniques).**

## Tips for Success

- **Consistency:** Practice these exercises daily to build long-term resilience and emotional balance.
- **Focus:** Pay attention to how your body and mind respond to each component of the exercises.
- **Customization:** Adjust the duration and intensity of the techniques to suit your needs.

By integrating these NeuroSomatic exercises into your routine, you can effectively manage stress, enhance focus, and promote emotional and physical well-being.

# WALKING GROUNDING WITH VAGUS NERVE ACTIVATION

**Purpose:** This exercise combines mindful movement, breath focus, and vagus nerve stimulation to reduce anxiety, enhance emotional regulation, and ground you in the present moment.

1. **Walk Slowly and Mindfully:** Focus on each step as you move.

2. **Incorporate Deep Breathing:** Practice slow belly breathing as you walk.

3. **Add Gentle Humming:** Hum softly with each exhale to stimulate your vagus nerve.

4. **Use Biofeedback:** Track your HRV to monitor emotional regulation in real time.

5. **Stay Present:** Focus on the sensation of walking and breathing to ground yourself in the moment.

6. **Repeat Until Calm:** Continue until you feel grounded and relaxed.

# DEEP BELLY BREATHING WITH PHYSICAL GROUNDING

**Purpose:** This exercise quickly alleviates stress and anxiety by anchoring you through physical grounding while calming your nervous system with deep, steady breathing.

1. Stand barefoot or sit with feet flat to connect with the ground.

2. Breathe deeply, expanding your belly as you inhale and relaxing it as you exhale.

3. Focus on physical sensations like stability and anchoring.

4. Use a biofeedback device to monitor HRV and adjust breathing for calmness.

5. **Repeat until calm;** practice regularly to improve stress management.

# WORKSHEET: NEUROSOMATIC THERAPY – WALKING GROUNDING WITH VNS & DEEP BREATHING

This worksheet guides you through two NeuroSomatic exercises to reduce anxiety, improve emotional regulation, and promote grounding. Combining mindful movement, deep breathing, physical grounding, and HRV biofeedback, these practices are designed to help you achieve a state of calm and focus.

| Date | Time of Session | HRV Device Used | Baseline HRV Reading |
|------|-----------------|-----------------|----------------------|
|      |                 |                 |                      |

## EXERCISE 1: WALKING GROUNDING WITH VAGUS NERVE ACTIVATION

### Environment Details

Where are you walking? (e.g., park, sidewalk, indoors).

What steps did you take to prepare? (e.g., comfortable shoes, quiet space).

### Mindful Walking Observations

What did you notice about each step? (e.g., the sensation of your feet touching the ground).

Did mindful walking help you feel more present? (e.g., yes, somewhat, not yet).

## Breathing and Humming

Describe your breathing rhythm as you walked. (e.g., steady, shallow, deep).

How did the humming affect your relaxation? (e.g., calming, neutral).

### HRV Feedback
How did your HRV change during this exercise? (e.g., increased coherence, no change).

## Outcome

How did you feel emotionally after walking? (e.g., less anxious, more focused).

How did you feel physically after walking? (e.g., lighter, more grounded).

## EXERCISE 2: DEEP BELLY BREATHING WITH PHYSICAL GROUNDING

### Environment and Position

Where did you practice? (e.g., barefoot on grass, seated on a chair).

How did you feel physically before starting? (e.g., tense, calm).

### Breathing Observations

How did your belly expand and contract during breathing? (e.g., fully, shallow).

Did you notice changes in your breath as you continued? (e.g., slower, deeper).

## Physical Grounding Sensations

> What did you notice about your connection to the ground or chair? (e.g., stability, warmth, relaxation).

> Did grounding help anchor your emotions? (e.g., yes, slightly, not yet).

> **HRV Feedback**
> How did your HRV respond to the exercise? (e.g., smoother patterns, steady improvement).

## Reflection and Outcomes

> **Which exercise felt more effective for you today? Why?**

## HRV Improvement

| Baseline HRV | Final HRV After Exercises | HRV Improvement |
|---|---|---|
| | | |

## Changes in Emotional and Physical State

| Emotional Shift: (e.g., from anxious to calm) | Physical Shift: (e.g., from tense to relaxed) |
|---|---|
| | |

## Reflection and Outcomes

> **Which techniques consistently lead to the most significant improvements in HRV or emotional balance?**

What adjustments will you make for future practice? (e.g., focus on a specific technique, combine exercises)

## WEEKLY SUMMARY (OPTIONAL)

| Date | Exercise Practiced | Duration | Baseline HRV | Post Session HRV | Emotional/Physical Observation |
|------|--------------------|----------|--------------|------------------|--------------------------------|
|      |                    |          |              |                  |                                |
|      |                    |          |              |                  |                                |

Adjustments for Future Sessions: What will you modify or try differently next time? (e.g., longer sessions, focus on specific techniques).

## Tips for Success

- **Consistency:** Practice daily or as needed to build long-term emotional resilience and physical stability.
- **Mindfulness:** Pay attention to the sensations in your body and your breathing rhythm to deepen your practice.
- **Customization:** Adjust the duration and intensity to suit your needs and track progress with HRV biofeedback for measurable results.
- By integrating these NeuroSomatic exercises into your routine, you can enhance emotional regulation, reduce anxiety, and ground yourself more effectively.

# COLD EXPOSURE WITH SOMATIC AWARENESS

**Purpose:** This exercise helps manage stress and hypervigilance by using cold exposure to stimulate the vagus nerve, paired with somatic awareness and controlled breathing to promote calmness and emotional resilience.

1. **Prepare for Cold Exposure:** Take a cold shower or immerse your face in cold water.
2. **Focus on Sensations:** Pay attention to how the cold feels on your skin.
3. **Maintain Controlled Breathing:** Practice deep, steady breaths to stay calm.
4. **Monitor HRV:** Track your HRV to observe how cold exposure affects your stress levels.
5. **Repeat Regularly:** This technique builds resilience and reduces stress over time.

## WORKSHEET: COLD EXPOSURE WITH SOMATIC AWARENESS

This worksheet helps you manage stress and hypervigilance by combining cold exposure, somatic awareness, and controlled breathing. The exercise stimulates the vagus nerve and promotes emotional resilience while allowing you to track your progress through HRV monitoring.

| Date | Time of Session | HRV Device Used | Baseline HRV Reading |
|---|---|---|---|
|  |  |  |  |

## STEP 1: PREPARE FOR COLD EXPOSURE

### Type of Cold Exposure Used

Cold Shower

Face Immersion in Cold Water

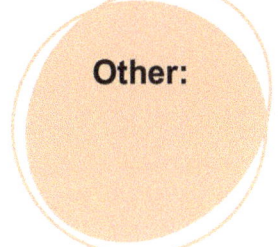

Other:

### Environment Details

| | | |
|---|---|---|
| Where are you practicing this technique? (e.g., bathroom, sink) | Initial Emotional State: (e.g., anxious, neutral, stressed) | Initial Physical State: (e.g., tense shoulders, elevated heart rate) |

## STEP 2: FOCUS ON SENSATIONS

### Sensory Observations During Cold Exposure

| How does the cold feel on your skin? (e.g., sharp, tingling, refreshing) | Which parts of your body reacted most to the cold? (e.g., face, hands, chest) |
|---|---|

Emotional Observations: How did the cold affect your emotional state? (e.g., heightened awareness, calming effect).

# STEP 3: MAINTAIN CONTROLLED BREATHING

### Breathing Observations

How steady was your breathing during the cold exposure? (e.g., smooth, shallow, controlled).

Did focusing on your breath help you stay calm? (e.g., yes, somewhat, not yet)

# STEP 4: MONITOR HRV

HRV Observations: Did your HRV change during or after the cold exposure? (e.g., steady improvement, no change).

### HRV Trends

| Baseline HRV | HRV After Cold Exposure |
|---|---|
| | |

# STEP 5: REFLECT ON THE EXPERIENCE

Physical Changes: How did your body feel after completing the cold exposure? (e.g., less tense, more energized)

Emotional Changes: How did your mood or emotional state change after the exercise? (e.g., calmer, focused, neutral)

Duration of Practice: How long did you sustain the cold exposure?

## Long-Term Tracking

> **Patterns Observed: Which part of the exercise (cold exposure, breathing, HRV monitoring) was most effective for reducing stress?**

> **Resilience Over Time: How has your ability to manage stress with this technique improved?**

> **Adjustments for Future Practice: What changes will you make to enhance this technique next time? (e.g., longer exposure, deeper focus on breathing)**

## WEEKLY SUMMARY (OPTIONAL)

| Date | Cold Exposure Method | Duration | Baseline HRV | Post Session HRV | Emotional/Physical Observation |
|------|----------------------|----------|--------------|------------------|-------------------------------|
|      |                      |          |              |                  |                               |

## Tips for Success

- **Start small:** Begin with shorter cold exposure times and gradually increase as you become more comfortable.
- **Focus on your breath:** Use deep, steady breathing to calm your body and mind during exposure.
- **Track your progress:** Monitor HRV and other personal changes to see how this technique builds resilience over time.
- By integrating cold exposure with somatic awareness into your routine, you can effectively reduce stress, enhance emotional regulation, and build long-term resilience.

# RESONANT BREATHING WITH BODY SCAN

**Purpose:** This exercise reduces stress and enhances relaxation by combining rhythmic breathing with a focused body scan, promoting greater body awareness and emotional balance.

1. **Find a Comfortable Position:** Sit or lie down where you can focus.
2. **Begin Resonant Breathing:** Inhale for five counts, hold briefly, and exhale for five counts.
3. **Perform a Body Scan:** Focus on each body part from head to toe, aligning the scan with your breath.
4. **Track Your HRV:** Use biofeedback to ensure a balanced, calming breath pattern.
5. **Relax and Reflect:** Note how this combination promotes relaxation and body awareness.

## WORKSHEET: RESONANT BREATHING WITH BODY SCAN

This worksheet guides you through a stress-reducing and relaxation-enhancing exercise by combining rhythmic breathing with a focused body scan. By promoting greater body awareness and emotional balance, this practice helps you manage stress effectively while monitoring your progress with HRV biofeedback.

| Date | Time of Session | HRV Device Used | Baseline HRV Reading |
|---|---|---|---|
|  |  |  |  |

# STEP 1: PREPARE FOR THE EXERCISE

| | |
|---|---|
| Comfortable Position: Are you sitting or lying down? (e.g., on a chair, yoga mat, recliner) | Environment: Describe your surroundings. (e.g., quiet room, dimmed lights, outdoors) |
| How do you feel emotionally before starting? (e.g., anxious, neutral, calm). | How does your body feel before starting? (e.g., tense shoulders, restless legs) |

# STEP 2: RESONANT BREATHING

## Breathing Pattern Observations

| | |
|---|---|
| How did inhaling for five counts and exhaling for five counts feel? (e.g., natural, slightly challenging) | Did you notice changes in your breathing rhythm as you continued? |

HRV Feedback (if applicable): How did your HRV respond during resonant breathing? (e.g., smoother coherence, slight fluctuations)

# STEP 3: PERFORM THE BODY SCAN

## Focus on Each Body Part

As you scanned from head to toe, what sensations did you notice?

| | |
|---|---|
| Head and Neck | |
| Shoulders and Arms | |
| Chest and Abdomen | |
| Legs and Feet | |

## Body Awareness

Were there areas of tension or discomfort that stood out?

How did focusing on your body change your awareness or relaxation level?

# STEP 4: REFLECT ON RELAXATION AND BODY AWARENESS

Physical Changes: How does your body feel after completing the exercise? (e.g., lighter, less tense)

Emotional Changes: How has your emotional state shifted? (e.g., calmer, more grounded)

## HRV Feedback

Final HRV Reading

Improvement from Baseline

# STEP 5: OVERALL REFLECTIONS

Did the combination of resonant breathing and body scan promote relaxation?

Very Effective

Moderately Effective

Slightly Effective

Not Effective

## Most Impactful Element

Which part of the exercise felt the most effective for you? (e.g., rhythmic breathing, focusing on specific body parts)

Challenges: Were there any parts of the exercise that were challenging or distracting? How will you address these next time?

Next Steps: How will you incorporate this practice into your routine? (e.g., daily, before stressful events)

## WEEKLY TRACKING SUMMARY (OPTIONAL)

| Date | Duration | Baseline HRV | Post Session HRV | Emotional/Physical Observation |
|------|----------|--------------|------------------|-------------------------------|
|      |          |              |                  |                               |

**Tips for Success**

- **Consistency:** Practice daily or as needed to reinforce the relaxation response and improve body awareness.
- **Mindfulness:** Focus on the sensations in your body and the rhythm of your breath for maximum impact.
- **Tracking Progress:** Use HRV biofeedback regularly to measure your progress and refine your practice.
- By regularly practicing resonant breathing with a body scan, you can achieve greater emotional balance, reduce stress, and develop a deeper connection with your body.

# TAI CHI MOVEMENTS WITH DIAPHRAGMATIC BREATHING AND HUMMING

> **Purpose:** This exercise improves flexibility, balance, and emotional regulation by integrating mindful movement, deep breathing, and vagus nerve stimulation to reduce anxiety and promote relaxation.

1. **Practice Slow Tai Chi Movements:** Focus on flowing, mindful movements.
2. **Add Deep Breathing:** Coordinate each movement with deep diaphragmatic breathing.
3. **Incorporate Humming:** Between movements, hum softly to activate the vagus nerve.
4. **Monitor Your HRV:** Use biofeedback to observe stress reduction and adjust your technique as needed.
5. **Repeat for Relaxation:** Continue until you feel calm and grounded

# WORKSHEET: TAI CHI WITH BREATHING AND HUMMING

> This worksheet guides you through a stress-reducing and relaxation-enhancing exercise by combining rhythmic breathing with a focused body scan. By promoting greater body awareness and emotional balance, this practice helps you manage stress effectively while monitoring your progress with HRV biofeedback.

## SESSION DETAILS

| Date | Time of Session | HRV Device Used | Baseline HRV Reading |
|------|-----------------|-----------------|----------------------|
|      |                 |                 |                      |

# STEP 1: PREPARE FOR TAI CHI PRACTICE

| Where are you practicing? (e.g., living room, garden, quiet studio) | How did you prepare the space? (e.g., cleared space, calming background music) |
|---|---|
| | |

| How do you feel emotionally before starting? (e.g., anxious, calm, neutral) | How does your body feel before starting? (e.g., stiff, balanced, tense) |
|---|---|
| | |

# STEP 2: PRACTICE SLOW TAI CHI MOVEMENTS

## Movement Observations

| How did your movements feel during practice? (e.g., flowing, deliberate, unsteady) | Were you able to focus on the flow of your movements? (e.g., yes, somewhat, not yet) |
|---|---|
| | |

Body Awareness: What physical sensations did you notice during the movements? (e.g., stretching, improved balance).

# STEP 3: ADD DEEP DIAPHRAGMATIC BREATHING

## Breathing Coordination

| How well did your breathing synchronize with your movements? (e.g., natural, challenging) | Did diaphragmatic breathing help enhance your focus or relaxation? |
|---|---|
| | |

**HRV Feedback (if applicable)**

| What changes in HRV did you notice while coordinating breathing and movement? (e.g., smoother coherence, no change) |
| --- |
| |

# STEP 4: INCORPORATE HUMMING

## Vagus Nerve Stimulation

| How did humming between movements feel? (e.g., soothing, calming vibrations) | What physical or emotional changes did you notice with humming? (e.g., reduced tension, improved focus) |
| --- | --- |
| | |

## HRV Feedback During Humming

| Did humming impact your HRV patterns? (e.g., steadier rhythm, increased variability) |
| --- |
| |

# STEP 5: REFLECT ON THE EXPERIENCE

| Overall Relaxation: How relaxed and grounded did you feel after completing the session? (e.g., very calm, somewhat relaxed) | Physical Outcomes: How does your body feel after practicing Tai Chi with breathing and humming? (e.g., more flexible, less tense) |
| --- | --- |
| | |

## HRV Feedback During Humming

| Emotional Outcomes: How has your mood or emotional state shifted? (e.g., calmer, more balanced) |
| --- |
| |

## HRV Summary

| Final HRV Reading | Improvement from Baseline |
|---|---|
|  |  |

## REFLECTION AND NEXT STEPS

How effective was this exercise in improving your physical and emotional state?

☐ Very Effective          ☐ Moderately Effective

☐ Slightly Effective      ☐ Not Effective

**Most Impactful Element: Which component of the exercise felt most beneficial? (e.g., movements, breathing, humming)**

**Challenges and Adjustments: Did you encounter any challenges during the session? How will you adjust next time?**

**Plan for Future Practice: How will you incorporate this exercise into your routine? (e.g., daily practice, stress relief after work)**

# WEEKLY TRACKING SUMMARY (OPTIONAL)

| Date | Duration | Baseline HRV | Post Session HRV | Emotional/Physical Observation |
|------|----------|--------------|------------------|-------------------------------|
|      |          |              |                  |                               |
|      |          |              |                  |                               |
|      |          |              |                  |                               |
|      |          |              |                  |                               |
|      |          |              |                  |                               |

## Tips for Success

- **Consistency:** Practice Tai Chi with diaphragmatic breathing and humming regularly to build long-term resilience and emotional balance.

- **Focus on Flow:** Allow your movements to guide your breath, creating a harmonious rhythm.

- **Track Progress:** Use HRV feedback to fine-tune your technique and measure improvement over time.

- By integrating this exercise into your routine, you can enhance flexibility, balance, and emotional regulation while promoting relaxation and reducing anxiety.

# INTEGRATED APPROACHES IN NEUROSOMATIC TRAUMA THERAPY

Trauma isn't just a mental experience—it's stored in the body, too. The burden of past wounds might persist, causing tense muscles, affecting your posture, and even impacting how you feel. If you've ever felt stuck, as if your body is holding onto something you can't quite let go of, you're not alone. The good news? There is a way to address both the mind and the body in healing trauma, and that's where Integrated NeuroSomatic Trauma Therapy comes in.

This technique combines two powerful modalities: somatic therapy, which focuses on the body's physical reaction to stress and previous experiences, and neuroscience, which helps us understand the brain's role in trauma. Combined, they provide a thorough healing process that tackles the underlying causes of trauma, enabling your body and mind to recover and become resilient.

Think of trauma like a knot in a rope. The knot still affects the entire length of the rope, regardless of how many times you untie the mental portion of it. However, the knot starts to relax when you start to untie the body and mind simultaneously, treating the emotional charge and releasing physical strain. This is what an integrated approach is all about: you're healing the body and mind together, not just separately.

Imagine when you were triggered, possibly experiencing a strong emotional reaction that appeared disproportionate to the circumstances. To release the stored trauma, picture combining that emotional therapy with body-based techniques like deep breathing, movement, or touch. Treating the physical and emotional parts of your experience can build a more successful and long-lasting holistic approach to healing.

This exercise will help you release trauma and achieve balance and safety by examining various integrated strategies. In addition to promoting emotional healing, these techniques will help you retrain your body and mind to react more skillfully to stress, trauma, and triggers. This integrative method encourages you to experience healing on all levels by restoring balance between the mind and body.

# GROUNDING WITH DIAPHRAGMATIC BREATHING AND HRV BIOFEEDBACK

**Purpose:** This exercise helps reduce hypervigilance, manage stress, and promote relaxation by combining grounding techniques, deep breathing, and real-time biofeedback.

1. **Find a Grounded Position:** Stand barefoot on the ground or hold a comforting object in your hands to create a sense of stability and connection.

2. **Begin Deep Belly Breathing:** Inhale deeply through your nose, expanding your abdomen as you breathe in. Exhale slowly through your mouth, allowing your belly to relax fully.

3. **Incorporate Humming:** As you exhale, hum softly to stimulate the vagus nerve and enhance relaxation.

4. **Use HRV Biofeedback:** Monitor your HRV using a biofeedback device to track your stress levels in real-time. Adjust your breathing rhythm to maintain a calm and steady pattern, focusing on smoother HRV readings.

5. **Repeat and Anchor Calmness:** Continue this exercise until you feel a reduction in hypervigilance and stress. Practice regularly to manage stress, promote physical recovery, and improve resilience to trauma.

## WORKSHEET: NEUROSOMATIC THERAPY GROUNDING WITH DIAPHRAGMATIC BREATHING AND HRV BIOFEEDBACK

This worksheet supports the reduction of hypervigilance, stress, and tension by integrating grounding techniques, deep diaphragmatic breathing, and real-time HRV biofeedback. By practicing regularly, you can promote relaxation, enhance vagus nerve activation, and improve resilience to trauma.

## SESSION DETAILS

| Date | Time of Session | HRV Device Used | Baseline HRV Reading |
|------|-----------------|-----------------|----------------------|
|      |                 |                 |                      |

## STEP 1: FIND A GROUNDED POSITION

Position Details: Are you standing barefoot, holding a comforting object, or using another grounding method? (e.g., seated with feet flat).

Initial Physical Sensations: What sensations do you notice as you connect to the ground or object? (e.g., warmth, texture, stability).

Initial Emotional State: How do you feel emotionally before starting? (e.g., anxious, neutral, calm).

## STEP 2: BEGIN DEEP BELLY BREATHING

### Breathing Observations

How does your abdomen move as you breathe deeply? (e.g., rising smoothly, shallow)

Are you able to focus on slow, steady breaths? (e.g., yes, somewhat, not yet)

HRV Feedback: How did your HRV respond to your breathing rhythm? (e.g., smoother pattern, slight fluctuations).

189

# STEP 3: INCORPORATE HUMMING

## Humming Observations

Describe the sensation of humming during exhalation. (e.g., soothing vibrations, calming)

Did humming deepen your relaxation or focus? (e.g., yes, no, neutral)

HRV Feedback During Humming: Did your HRV improve while incorporating humming? (e.g., steadier rhythm, increased coherence)

# STEP 4: MONITOR HRV AND ADJUST

Real-Time HRV Observations: What trends did you observe in your HRV as you continued the exercise? (e.g., improvement, stable pattern).

Adjustments Made: Did you modify your breathing rhythm or grounding technique based on HRV feedback? (e.g., slowed exhale, adjusted posture)

# STEP 5: REPEAT AND ANCHOR CALMNESS

Duration of Practice: How long did you practice this exercise? (e.g., 5 minutes, 10 minutes).

Physical Changes: How does your body feel now compared to before? (e.g., less tense, more relaxed).

Emotional Changes: How has your emotional state shifted? (e.g., calmer, more balanced).

## Final HRV Reading

| | |
|---|---|
| **What was your HRV at the end of the session?** | **Improvement from Baseline** |

# REFLECTION AND NEXT STEPS

How effective was this practice in reducing stress or hypervigilance?

☐ Very Effective                    ☐ Moderately Effective

☐ Slightly Effective                ☐ Not Effective

**Most Impactful Component: Which aspect of the exercise felt the most beneficial? (e.g., grounding, breathing, humming, biofeedback).**

**Challenges and Adjustments: Did you face any challenges during the session? How will you address them next time?**

**Plan for Future Practice: How often will you incorporate this exercise into your routine? (e.g., daily, before stressful events)**

# WEEKLY TRACKING SUMMARY (OPTIONAL)

| Date | Duration | Baseline HRV | Post Session HRV | Emotional/Physical Observation |
|---|---|---|---|---|
|  |  |  |  |  |
|  |  |  |  |  |
|  |  |  |  |  |
|  |  |  |  |  |
|  |  |  |  |  |

## Tips for Success

- **Consistency:** Regular practice helps build long-term resilience and improves your ability to manage stress.
- **Focus:** Pay attention to your body and HRV feedback to fine-tune your technique for maximum relaxation.
- **Customization:** Adjust the grounding method or breathing rhythm to suit your preferences and needs.
- By practicing grounding with diaphragmatic breathing and HRV biofeedback, you can achieve greater emotional regulation, physical relaxation, and resilience to trauma.

# WORKSHEET: BODY SCAN WITH BREATHING AND VNS BIOFEEDBACK

This worksheet supports the management of PTSD symptoms by reducing physical tension and promoting relaxation through body awareness, resonant breathing, and vagus nerve stimulation. By practicing regularly, you can improve emotional regulation, manage trauma symptoms, and enhance overall well-being.

## SESSION DETAILS

| Date | Time of Session | HRV Device Used | Baseline HRV Reading |
|------|-----------------|-----------------|----------------------|
|      |                 |                 |                      |

## STEP 1: FIND A COMFORTABLE POSITION

| Environment: Where are you practicing? (e.g., quiet bedroom, yoga mat, recliner). | Initial Emotional State: How do you feel emotionally before starting? (e.g., anxious, neutral, overwhelmed). | Initial Physical State: How does your body feel before starting? (e.g., tense shoulders, tight jaw, restless legs). |
|---|---|---|
|   |   |   |

## STEP 2: BEGIN RESONANT BREATHING

### Breathing Rhythm

| Inhale deeply for 5 counts, hold briefly, and exhale slowly for 5 counts. | How did this breathing rhythm feel? (e.g., calming, challenging). |
|---|---|
|   |   |

## STEP 3: PERFORM A BODY SCAN

### Body Scan Observations

Focus on each part of your body, starting from your head and moving downward:

| | |
|---|---|
| **Head and Neck** | |
| **Shoulders and Arms** | |
| **Chest and Abdomen** | |
| **Legs and Feet** | |

### Releasing Tension

What areas of your body held the most tension?

How did you feel as you consciously released tension in those areas?

## STEP 4: INCORPORATE VOCAL HUMMING

How did humming during exhalation feel? (e.g., soothing vibrations, calming effect)

Did humming enhance your sense of relaxation? (e.g., yes, somewhat, neutral)

HRV Feedback During Humming: Did humming impact your HRV readings? (e.g., increased coherence, steady improvement)

## STEP 5: CONCLUDE WITH REFLECTION

Physical Changes: How does your body feel now compared to when you started? (e.g., lighter, less tense)

Emotional Changes: How has your emotional state shifted? (e.g., calmer, more grounded)

### HRV Improvement

Final HRV Reading

Improvement from Baseline

## STEP 6: OVERALL REFLECTIONS AND NEXT STEPS

**Effectiveness of the Exercise:** How effective was this practice in managing your PTSD symptoms or reducing tension?

Very Effective

Moderately Effective

Slightly Effective

Not Effective

| Most Impactful Component: Which part of the exercise felt most beneficial? (e.g., breathing, body scan, humming). | Challenges and Adjustments: Did you encounter any difficulties during the session? How will you address them next time? | Plan for Future Practice: How will you integrate this exercise into your routine? (e.g., daily practice, after triggering events). |
|---|---|---|
|  |  |  |

# WEEKLY TRACKING SUMMARY (OPTIONAL)

| Date | Duration | Baseline HRV | Post Session HRV | Emotional/Physical Observation |
|---|---|---|---|---|
|  |  |  |  |  |

## Tips for Success

- **Consistency:** Practice this technique regularly to reinforce your body's relaxation response and build resilience.
- **Focus:** Stay attentive to the sensations in your body and your HRV feedback for optimal results.
- **Adjustments:** Customize the exercise to suit your needs, such as focusing more on humming or scanning certain tense areas.
- By combining resonant breathing, body awareness, and vagus nerve stimulation, you can effectively manage PTSD symptoms and enhance your emotional and physical well-being.

# TAI CHI MOVEMENTS WITH COHERENT BREATHING AND VNS

**Purpose:** This exercise helps reduce anxiety, manage hyperarousal, and improve flexibility and balance by combining mindful movement, coherent breathing, and vagus nerve stimulation.

1. **Prepare for Tai Chi Practice:** Find a quiet space with enough room to move comfortably. Stand with your feet shoulder-width apart and your body relaxed.
2. **Practice Slow, Mindful Movements:** Perform gentle Tai Chi movements, focusing on smooth, flowing motions. Keep your movements slow and deliberate.
3. **Incorporate Coherent Breathing:** Coordinate your movements with deep, rhythmic breathing. Inhale for a count of four as you begin a movement, and exhale for a count of four as you complete it.
4. **Add Vocal Humming:** Between movements, hum softly during your exhale to stimulate the vagus nerve and enhance relaxation.
5. **Use HRV Biofeedback:** Track your HRV with a biofeedback device as you move and breathe. Adjust your technique as needed to maintain a calm, balanced state.
6. **Focus on Balance and Flexibility:** Pay attention to your body's alignment and muscles' feelings during each motion. Allow the exercise to improve your balance and range of motion over time.
7. **Repeat for Relaxation and Centering:** Continue practicing for 10–15 minutes until you feel calmer and more centered. Use this exercise regularly to manage anxiety and hyperarousal effectively.

# WORKSHEET: TAI CHI MOVEMENTS WITH COHERENT BREATHING AND VNS

This worksheet guides you through Tai Chi movements combined with coherent breathing and vagus nerve stimulation. Designed to reduce anxiety, manage hyperarousal, and improve flexibility and balance, this exercise uses HRV biofeedback to track progress and promote relaxation and emotional regulation.

## SESSION DETAILS

| Date | Time of Session | HRV Device Used | Baseline HRV Reading |
|------|-----------------|-----------------|----------------------|
|      |                 |                 |                      |

## STEP 1: PREPARE FOR TAI CHI PRACTICE

**Environment: Where are you practicing? (e.g., living room, garden, yoga studio)**

**Initial Emotional State: How do you feel emotionally before starting? (e.g., anxious, calm, distracted)**

**Initial Physical State: How does your body feel before starting? (e.g., tense, neutral, stiff)**

## STEP 2: PRACTICE SLOW, MINDFUL MOVEMENTS

### Movement Observations

**How did your movements feel during the session? (e.g., smooth, deliberate, unsteady)**

**Were there any areas of your body that felt tight or needed extra attention?**

**Focus on Alignment: How did you ensure your posture and alignment were correct during the movements? (e.g., standing tall, grounding feet)**

# STEP 3: INCORPORATE COHERENT BREATHING

How well did you coordinate your breathing with your movements? (e.g., natural, challenging)

Did the rhythm of inhaling for four counts and exhaling for four counts feel calming?

HRV Feedback During Breathing: What changes did you observe in your HRV while practicing coherent breathing? (e.g., steadier rhythm, smoother patterns)

# STEP 4: ADD VOCAL HUMMING

## Humming Observations

How did humming during exhalation feel? (e.g., calming vibrations, deep relaxation)

Did humming enhance your relaxation or focus? (e.g., yes, somewhat, neutral)

HRV Feedback During Humming: Did your HRV improve with humming? (e.g., higher coherence, steady improvement)

# STEP 5: FOCUS ON BALANCE AND FLEXIBILITY

## Physical Observations

Describe the sensation of humming during exhalation. (e.g., soothing vibrations, calming))

Did you notice any changes in your flexibility as you practiced?

**Alignment Awareness: How did focusing on your alignment and muscle engagement improve the exercise?**

# OVERALL REFLECTIONS AND NEXT STEPS

How effective was this practice in managing your anxiety or hyperarousal?

☐ Very Effective

☐ Moderately Effective

☐ Slightly Effective

☐ Not Effective

**Most Impactful Component: Which part of the exercise felt most beneficial? (e.g., movements, breathing, humming)**

**Challenges and Adjustments: Were there any challenges during the session? How will you address them next time?**

**Plan for Future Practice: How often will you integrate this exercise into your routine? (e.g., daily, after stressful events)**

# WEEKLY TRACKING SUMMARY (OPTIONAL)

| Date | Duration | Baseline HRV | Post Session HRV | Emotional/Physical Observation |
|------|----------|--------------|------------------|-------------------------------|
|      |          |              |                  |                               |
|      |          |              |                  |                               |
|      |          |              |                  |                               |
|      |          |              |                  |                               |
|      |          |              |                  |                               |

## Tips for Success

- **Consistency:** Practice daily or as needed to build resilience and manage stress effectively.
- **Focus on Flow:** Let your breathing and movements flow together harmoniously for maximum benefit.
- **Track Progress:** Use HRV biofeedback to monitor improvements over time and refine your technique.
- By integrating mindful movements, coherent breathing, and vagus nerve stimulation into your routine, you can effectively reduce anxiety, improve balance, and promote relaxation.

# COLD EXPOSURE WITH GROUNDING AND DIAPHRAGMATIC BREATHING

**Purpose:** This exercise helps manage hypervigilance, reduce inflammation, and improve mental and physical recovery by combining cold exposure, grounding techniques, diaphragmatic breathing, and vagus nerve stimulation.

1. **Prepare for Cold Exposure:** Choose a method of cold exposure, such as a cold shower or immersing your face in cold water.
2. **Engage in Physical Grounding:** Stand barefoot on the ground or hold a textured object to anchor yourself physically and mentally.
3. **Begin Diaphragmatic Breathing:** Inhale deeply through your nose, expanding your belly as you breathe in. Exhale slowly through your mouth, focusing on steady, controlled breathing.
4. **Incorporate Vocal Humming:** During each exhale, hum softly to stimulate the vagus nerve and enhance relaxation.
5. **Use HRV Biofeedback:** Monitor your HRV with a biofeedback device to track your body's response to cold exposure. Adjust your breathing to maintain a calm, balanced state.
6. **Focus on Sensations:** Pay attention to the sensations of the cold on your skin and how your body responds. Use this awareness to stay grounded in the present moment.
7. **Conclude and Reflect:** End the cold exposure session after 1–3 minutes or when you feel ready. Take a moment to notice the changes in your stress levels and how your body feels.
8. **Repeat this Exercise:** Repeat regularly to build resilience and enhance your overall mental and physical health.

# WORKSHEET: COLD EXPOSURE WITH GROUNDING AND DIAPHRAGMATIC BREATHING

This worksheet guides you through a trauma-informed exercise that combines cold exposure, grounding techniques, diaphragmatic breathing, and vagus nerve stimulation to manage hypervigilance, reduce inflammation, and promote recovery. By monitoring HRV biofeedback, you can track your body's response and improve resilience over time.

## SESSION DETAILS

| Date | Time of Session | HRV Device Used | Baseline HRV Reading |
|------|-----------------|-----------------|----------------------|
|      |                 |                 |                      |

## STEP 1: PREPARE FOR COLD EXPOSURE

Cold Exposure Method: What method did you choose for cold exposure? (e.g., cold shower, face immersion in cold water)

Preparation Details: How did you prepare for the session? (e.g., set timer, towel nearby)

## STEP 2: ENGAGE IN PHYSICAL GROUNDING

Grounding Technique: Are you standing barefoot or holding a textured object? (e.g., barefoot on grass, holding a stress ball)

Initial Observations: How do you feel physically and mentally before starting? (e.g., tense, anxious, neutral)

## STEP 3: BEGIN DIAPHRAGMATIC BREATHING

Breathing Observations: How does your belly expand and contract with each breath? (e.g., smooth, shallow, rhythmic)

Did focusing on your breathing help you feel calmer? (e.g., yes, somewhat, no)

# STEP 4: INCORPORATE VOCAL HUMMING

## Humming Observations

Describe the sensations during humming. (e.g., vibrations in chest or throat, calming effect)

Did humming enhance your relaxation or focus? (e.g., yes, somewhat, no)

**HRV Feedback During Humming:** How did your HRV respond to humming? (e.g., steady improvement, no change)

# STEP 5: FOCUS ON SENSATIONS

## Cold Sensations

How did the cold feel on your skin? (e.g., sharp, invigorating, numbing)

Were you able to stay present with the sensations without becoming overwhelmed? (e.g., yes, somewhat, no)

**Body Awareness:** How did your body respond to the cold? (e.g., tensing, relaxing, neutral)

# STEP 6: CONCLUDE AND REFLECT

| | | |
|---|---|---|
| **Duration of Cold Exposure: How long did you sustain the cold exposure? (e.g., 1 minute, 2 minutes)** | **Changes in Physical and Emotional State: How do you feel physically after the session? (e.g., less tense, energized)** | **How do you feel emotionally after the session? (e.g., calmer, more grounded)** |

## HRV Feedback Summary

| **Final HRV Reading** | **Improvement from Baseline** |
|---|---|
| | |

# STEP 7: REPEAT AND BUILD RESILIENCE

How effective was this session in reducing stress or hypervigilance?

- [ ] Very Effective
- [ ] Moderately Effective
- [ ] Slightly Effective
- [ ] Not Effective

| | |
|---|---|
| **Challenges and Adjustments: Were there any challenges during the session? How will you address them next time?** | **Plan for Future Practice: How often will you integrate this exercise into your routine? (e.g., daily, as needed)** |

# WEEKLY TRACKING SUMMARY (OPTIONAL)

| Date | Duration | Baseline HRV | Post Session HRV | Emotional/Physical Observation |
|---|---|---|---|---|
| | | | | |
| | | | | |
| | | | | |
| | | | | |
| | | | | |

## Tips for Success

- **Start Small:** Begin with shorter exposure times and gradually increase as you become more comfortable.

- **Focus on Breathing:** Use diaphragmatic breathing and humming to stay relaxed and grounded.

- **Track Progress:** Regularly monitor your HRV and observe patterns in your physical and emotional responses.

- By practicing cold exposure with grounding and diaphragmatic breathing, you can effectively manage hypervigilance, reduce stress, and improve mental and physical resilience.

# PMR WITH GUIDED IMAGERY AND VNS

**Purpose:** This exercise helps reduce muscle tension, enhance emotional stability, and manage PTSD symptoms by combining PMR, guided imagery, and vagus nerve stimulation.

1. **Find a Comfortable Position:** Sit or lie down in a quiet, comfortable space where you can focus without distractions.

2. **Begin Progressive Muscle Relaxation (PMR):** Start with your feet, tensing each muscle group for a few seconds before slowly releasing the tension. Gradually move upward through your body, focusing on one muscle group at a time, ending with your shoulders and jaw.

3. **Incorporate Guided Imagery:** As you relax each muscle group, visualize a safe, calming place like a beach, forest, or cozy room. Engage your senses by imagining this safe space's sights, sounds, and feelings.

4. **Add Vocal Humming:** During each exhale, hum softly to stimulate the vagus nerve and deepen relaxation.

5. **Use HRV Biofeedback (Optional):** Monitor your HRV with a biofeedback device to observe the calming effects and adjust your breathing for optimal relaxation.

6. **Complete the Session:** Once you have relaxed all muscle groups, spend a moment fully immersed in your safe space visualization. Reflect on the calmness and sense of stability you have achieved.

7. **Repeat Regularly:** Practice this exercise daily or whenever you experience heightened stress or PTSD symptoms to promote relaxation and emotional stability.

# WORKSHEET: PMR WITH GUIDED IMAGERY AND VNS

This worksheet supports the reduction of muscle tension and emotional stress by integrating Progressive Muscle Relaxation (PMR), guided imagery, and vagus nerve stimulation. Designed to manage PTSD symptoms and enhance emotional stability, this exercise combines physical relaxation with mental imagery and biofeedback for maximum effectiveness.

## SESSION DETAILS

| Date | Time of Session | HRV Device Used | Baseline HRV Reading |
|---|---|---|---|
| | | | |

## STEP 1: FIND A COMFORTABLE POSITION

| | | |
|---|---|---|
| **Environment:** Where are you practicing? (e.g., quiet bedroom, yoga mat, recliner) | **Initial Emotional State:** How do you feel emotionally before starting? (e.g., anxious, calm, overwhelmed) | **Initial Physical State:** How does your body feel before starting? (e.g., tense shoulders, tight jaw, restless legs) |

# STEP 2: PROGRESSIVE MUSCLE RELAXATION (PMR)

**Tension and Relaxation Observations:** How did tensing and releasing each muscle group feel?

| | |
|---|---|
| **Arms and Hands** | |
| **Shoulders, Neck, and Jaw** | |
| **Abdomen and Chest** | |
| **Legs and Feet** | |

| | |
|---|---|
| **Body Awareness:** Did you notice areas of your body holding more tension than others? | **HRV Feedback (if applicable):** How did your HRV readings change during PMR? (e.g., steady improvement, slight fluctuation) |

# STEP 3: INCORPORATE GUIDED IMAGERY

Visualize a Safe Place: What safe, calming place did you imagine? (e.g., beach, forest, cozy room)

Relaxation Observations: How did focusing on your safe space affect your emotional and physical state?

## Engage Your Senses

What did you see?

What did you hear?

What did you feel? (e.g., warmth, breeze, softness)

# STEP 4: REPEAT REGULARLY

How effective was this session in managing PTSD symptoms or reducing tension?

- Very Effective
- Moderately Effective
- Slightly Effective
- Not Effective

# STEP 5: ADD VOCAL HUMMING

## Humming Observations

How did humming during exhalation feel? (e.g., soothing vibrations, deep relaxation)

Did humming enhance your sense of calmness or stability?

HRV Feedback During Humming: Did humming impact your HRV readings? (e.g., increased coherence, steady improvement)

# STEP 6: COMPLETE THE SESSION

**Immersion in Safe Space:** How did it feel to spend time fully immersed in your visualization after relaxing your body?

**Reflection on Calmness:** What changes did you notice in your stress levels or emotional state? (e.g., calmer, more grounded)

**What was your HRV at the end of the session?**

**Improvement from Baseline**

**Most Impactful Component:** Which part of the exercise felt most beneficial? (e.g., PMR, guided imagery, humming)

**Challenges and Adjustments:** Were there any challenges during the session? How will you address them next time?

**Plan for Future Practice:** How often will you integrate this exercise into your routine? (e.g., daily, as needed)

# WEEKLY TRACKING SUMMARY (OPTIONAL)

| Date | Duration | Baseline HRV | Post Session HRV | Emotional/Physical Observation |
|---|---|---|---|---|
| | | | | |
| | | | | |
| | | | | |
| | | | | |
| | | | | |

## Tips for Success

- **Consistency:** Practice regularly to reinforce relaxation and emotional stability.
- **Engage Your Senses:** Fully immerse yourself in your safe space visualization for maximum effectiveness.
- **Track Progress:** Use HRV biofeedback to monitor improvements over time and refine your technique.
- By combining PMR, guided imagery, and vagus nerve stimulation, you can effectively manage PTSD symptoms, reduce stress, and promote long-term emotional and physical well-being.

# END-BOOK REVIEW PAGE

## Got a Minute?

You've reached the end of the book, but your journey is far from over, and the techniques you've learned here will continue to serve you for the rest of your life. Please take a moment now to share them with the wider world.

By sharing your honest opinion of this book and a little about how it's helped you, you'll show new readers exactly where they can find it and help them feel the changes in their own lives, too.

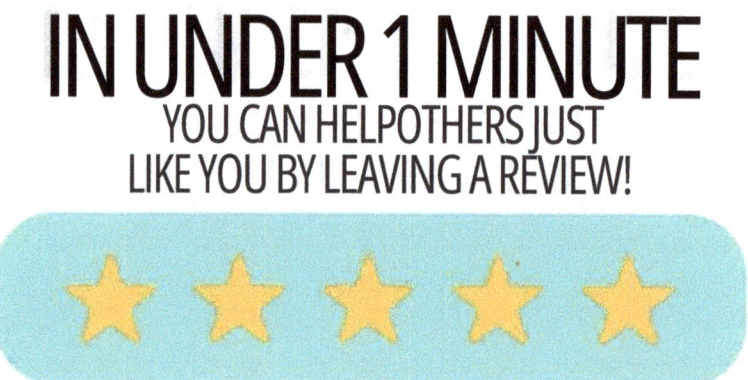

**IN UNDER 1 MINUTE**
YOU CAN HELP OTHERS JUST
LIKE YOU BY LEAVING A REVIEW!

Thank you so much for your support. This workbook will be here for you whenever you need it-revisit it as often as you like, and continue to use somatic therapy to keep you grounded and in control of your emotional experience.

>>> **S**can **QR** Co**d**e to leave your review on Amazon.

# CONCLUSION

**C**ongratulations! You've made it to the end of this workbook, and that's something worth celebrating. Take a moment to recognize the effort you've put into this journey. Showing up for yourself, even in small ways, is no small feat.

By now, you've explored a variety of somatic exercises, practiced tuning into your body's signals, and learned how to use vagus nerve stimulation and heart rate variability biofeedback to support your mental and emotional health. These tools aren't just temporary fixes—they're lifelong skills you can rely on when navigating stress, anxiety, or even just the ups and downs of daily life.

**Remember,** this isn't about perfection. It's about progress. Healing and personal growth don't follow a straight line. There will be days when these practices feel easy and natural and other days when it feels like a struggle to start. That's okay. What matters most is that you keep returning to these tools and trusting the process.

Think of this workbook as your foundation. You've built something solid here—something you can lean on whenever needed. Whether working through past traumas, managing anxiety, or striving to feel more connected to yourself and the world, these techniques are here for you.

I want you to experiment and discover what works best as you progress. Maybe it's starting your morning with deep breaths and gentle movement or using biofeedback to calm yourself before a big event. Whatever your path looks like, know that you have the power to shape it. Thank you for trusting this workbook to be part of your healing journey. I hope it's been as transformative for you as it was meant to be. You've got this—one moment, one breath, and one step at a time.

**Here's to a healthier, happier, and more resilient you!**

# DEEPEN YOUR SOMATIC THERAPY KNOWLEDGE

If you've found value in this workbook, the next step is expanding your understanding of the science and principles behind the practices.

## Simple Somatic Therapy Solution – The Main Book

You can go beyond the exercises with the full guide that explains how and why somatic therapy, vagus nerve stimulation, and HRV biofeedback work. This foundational book offers the insights, neuroscience, and step-by-step guidance to empower your healing journey from the inside out.

## More Titles Coming Soon

We're growing the series to support deeper emotional resilience, trauma recovery, and nervous system health for teens, parents, professionals, and anyone seeking real, lasting change.

## Explore More with Holistic Harmony Publications

Find free resources, guided tools, and upcoming releases at: www.HolisticHarmonyPublications.com

## Browse All Our Books on Amazon

Check out our full catalog at the Holistic Harmony Publications Amazon author page:

**amazon.com/Holistic-Harmony-Publications**

www.ingramcontent.com/pod-product-compliance
Lightning Source LLC
Chambersburg PA
CBHW041113120626
46547CB00019B/2691